A new rhetoric

Essays on using the internet to communicate

R.E. Stewart

R.E. Stewart

Contents

A new rhetoric: essays on using the internet to communicate

"Now to plain dealing. Lay these glozes by.
Shall we resolve to woo these girls of France?"

\-   *Love's Labour*'s *Lost*, William Shakespeare

A new rhetoric: essays on using the internet to communicate

Introduction

The "painted flourish"

A new rhetoric: essays on using the internet to communicate

"I suffer for the truth," says the rustic Costard in Shakespeare's *Love's Labour's Lost*. In a kingdom which has, on pain of imprisonment, abjured all consort with the fairer sex, he has just been taken "in manner and form" with Jaquenetta, a country wench. The "truth" for which poor Costard suffers is double-edged: the fact of his offence, and the reality which the King's unrealistic laws debar. The punishment is swiftly commuted to a week on bran and water. And so this comical vignette contains and foreshadows the central problem which leaves more or less everyone in the play "forsworn".

The status, not just the language, of *Love's Labour's Lost* is ambiguous. Outwardly, it is a comedy. The King of Navarre and three attending lords withdraw from the world and publicly mortify all bodily things, including the company of women. Instead they will steep their minds in the philosophical life of study, language and learning. But as soon as all of this is enshrined in law, it collides with a world all too inconveniently real. The King is straight away in a diplomatic tangle, when he recalls that the King of France's daughter – with a retinue of ladies – approaches, apparently to conduct a territorial negotiation.

The comic conceit of the play is almost contrived to place the polar forces of gender hand in hand, while making fun of high-minded hypocrisy. That, at least, is how a comedy might play out, and for much of its turns of wit and effusive language the audience, but for the play's title, is led to believe that it will end much as any other "old play". But the abrupt, almost indifferently rude, news of a death in the final furlong and the stony, disbelieving silence that ensues, leaves us to digest the shock conclusion that "Jack hath not Jill". We then begin to grasp that there is a hint of something tragic going on: scholarly renunciation only creates the conditions in which life too easily slips through your fingers.

If the Kingdom of Navarre takes flight from the world, it is clear from the play that it alights on the gushing air of too much tongue. Words run feral and untamed from one character to another, unable to take their cue from a well-judged circumstance and certainly incapable of well-judged silence. Love is no less a cue to which this language won't respond. "Beauty", says the French princess, "needs not the painted flourish of your praise." And to drive the point home, it is not bought by the "base sale of chapmen's tongues." Biron, the dimly discerning voice of reason at the King's court, recognises this, albeit too late, and enjoins his peers to forswear their oaths as ultimately it "is religion to be thus forsworn".

The language of persuasion – *rhetoric* – is, in the play, a farcically camped-up tragicomic dame, which is, for all its painted flourishes, eluded by reality. This, at its simplest, tells us that it is a poor form of rhetoric; that it does *not* persuade. True rhetoric starts from properly engaging with reality, from the nature of something that might *admit* persuasion. Spying this well-worn grain throughout the play, A.D Nuttall suggests that there is something ethical at work in Shakespeare's mind, and even proposes that he is scribbling guilt about his own intelligence:

"He grasps the psychological truth that even if words are variously engaged with the extra-verbal world, we can, by a trick of the mind, focus on the formal expression and so lose full engagement, even while we are applauding our own cleverness. Of this he is ashamed."

The unifying thought, if not the carefully cropped argument, of these essays is that the current state of digital rhetoric, or "digital communications", is similar to the problems of Shakespeare's play. The language of *Love's Labour's Lost* is, in the jargon, "nominalist"; words are true in name only, severed from any root in the "real" world. Digital communications might start from a different place, but are they any more real?

Most digital rhetoric, like the place of rhetoric in the play, sets out to persuade: it wants someone to cough up some cash for something, to read or watch something, to engage with something and give their view. So the focus of creating anything online usually crystallises around whatever the goal might be. The language, the design, the multimedia are instruments designed to capture the attention of "users" and channel them towards the intended goal. In the language of digital marketing, when this goal is achieved we call it a "conversion". To sand it down to its smoothest, digital rhetoric is, for the most part, "practical".

The corollaries of this "practical" character have produced ever-changing rules or industry-standard guidance about how to communicate effectively. Such rules cover, variously, how to write a piece of text for the way people read in a web browser, the appropriate length for an online video, how to write headlines and introductory text given the different ways they might appear across digital networks, how to "optimise" web pages for search engines, how to plan and govern the creation of digital content … and so on. Guidance and consultancy is now a considerable industry in its own right.

All of this might, at face value, look very different from the matters which lend dramatic tension to *Love's Labour's Lost*. But, to desecrate the richness of Shakespeare's language, a "conversion" in the plot of the play would, unlike its actual ending, see that Jack has his Jill. The play's protagonists do not "convert" their goal, because the language of persuasion is a character in its own right, one that does not render service to anyone or anything; it pirouettes to futile exhaustion. We might see similar "painted flourishes" online, but generally things tend to be more utilitarian: users want to do "x" so we will allow them to do it by designing "y". This might be less florid, but it doesn't make it any more human. Just as the laborious language of love cannot sit still long enough to observe and celebrate the object of its admiration, digital rhetoric defaults to a mechanical habit of thought which more or less blindly ignores the fact that people are more than brains in jars who want to "maximise" their choices.

I have given the "user experience" more than a few mentions in what follows, not because I claim to explore or illuminate it in fresh new ways. My knowledge of it - and "user-centred design" - is based on practical knowledge of managing digital content. I have held, at the most, a sort of dilettantish VIP ticket which has allowed me to see the professionals at work. But, with that caveat, the user experience seems to me to reflect a critical change and new momentum in the development of digital communications.

The history runs something like this: in the beginning there were websites built by people who understood the newfangled technologies that made them possible. People who used the websites struggled, so, in much the same way that in the early days of film the studios screen-tested daily footage, we started to put models in front of people and tested how easy or difficult they found them to use. Out of such "usability testing" came a startling revelation: people don't stop behaving like human beings when you ask them to operate a computer; they respond not just rationally but *emotionally*. So the goal when designing websites or online applications has since become to create a pleasurable, even desirable, all round experience.

You might précis all of this by saying that the "user experience" is artificial intelligence telling itself that it needs to be more than artificially intelligent. By posing an entirely practical and utilitarian question, the new church of the user experience enjoins us to celebrate more than our, arguably overstated, capacity for level-headed judgement. Instead we need to discover a little more character and personality. It is, perhaps, a mark of just how far this thought is only incipient that "character and personality" tend to share in a fairly blunt and homogenous identity. The most noticeable character traits of "digital content" with personality often resemble the kind of conversations you might expect to hear at a Californian beach party. Still, I am sure Californian beach parties qualify as human activities.

Another way in which the robot is telling itself to acquire human characteristics is the high-pitched preoccupation with the importance of "content" among many digital marketing professionals. We are told again and again that sites must create, and crucially plan, "high quality" content because "content is king". This now flies under the flag of "content strategy", a handle which, not unlike the pullulating use of the word "content", sounds a little like a software programme for overcoming the limitations of software programmes.

This means that, even as they pioneer new ways of doing things, the "user experience" and "content strategy" can look a lot like rationalisations which signal an important shift in the use of the internet, but which have not fully overcome the mindset they are in the process of deconstructing. They want to make the internet speak to something more vital and human than a score. But they still talk as though "content", like "rhetoric" in *Love's Labour's Lost*, is a sort of unhinged entity in its own right, which requires a method or skillset to master it. When, in fact, good content begins mysteriously, and often elusively, in the heartbeat of living things under particular circumstances. To be a master of "content" is to be nothing more than a pedlar of cheap tricks. Good digital communication, like any good communication, must combine a knowledge, interest and respect for *something* – art, acupuncture, line-dancing, wildlife etc – with mastery of the new tool.

The clamour around the user experience and content strategy suggest that the internet is, with bovine movement, discovering a hopeful trajectory, and one that is hopeful not just for the technology, but, in a more attenuated sense, for people and human culture. The technology has brokered radically new ways of interrogating and interacting with the world around us, unleashing new potential, perspectives, ideas and experiences, but we have not quite managed to wrestle all of this into a shape which suits the crooked and idiosyncratic character of human nature. This means that digital communications are in a state of discovery and creative tension between a view of the world as a sort of blunt-edged technical calculus and one that ushers and persuades the unpredictable character and animus of things.

The three essays in this volume survey different aspects of this tension. The first asks what it might mean if the internet were to truly enthrone "content"; the second and third consider the matter from respectively the perspectives of art and politics.

The essays, at a deeper level, imply that there is something in the virtual pulse of the internet which wants to challenge more than the thought-patterns of machines. The utilitarian, technocratic frame of mind, which wants to reduce everything to a matrix of determinate calculations, reaches backwards beyond the accidental development of a technological revolution in the 1990s.

The German philosopher, Martin Heidegger, among his later writings famously wrote, with deliberate and gnomic disguise, about the question of technology, and described the "essence of technology" as the central question in a tradition of thought reaching back to the ancient world. Heidegger has a word for how the "technocratic frame of mind" thinks about the world; he calls it *Bestand*, usually translated as "standing-reserve", but sometimes as "resource". Technology is not simply a helpful tool, but a "mode of knowing" or a way of characterising things, in this case by shaping them or "enframing" them as an instrument trans-figured to serve some quantifiable purpose. This frame of mind, which for Heidegger permeates all habits of thought in the modern world and not just science and technology, construes things in the same way a hydroelectric engineer "understands" a river.

At one level, of course, a hydroelectric engineer *does* understand rivers. Heidegger's point seems to be that there is something unilateral and purblind about making this the only way to characterise them. All of which circles back to something that any right-minded reflection on the mercenary uses of rhetoric might hope to avoid: truth.

It might, to modern ears, look like an eccentric starting point, but, like many of his extended meditations, Heidegger's thoughts about truth begin by examining the meaning of the word in ancient Greek; and out of this meaning he revises a way forward. The Greek word – *alētheia* – properly translated has the meaning "being unconcealed". Truth is a sort of making manifest, uncovering, unconcealment. Among his other reflections, by this light, he characterises art not as creating something new, but unveiling or discovering a phenomenon in its original light. Whatever light a great work of art harnesses, however, it is limited or concealed, just like the world as construed by technology, by the figure or frame in which it hangs. This leads Heidegger to make the sort of statement which gives continental philosophy a bad name: that "truth is untruth". We discern truth through a process of unconcealment, one which is nevertheless limited by the edges of the figure which brings it forth.

The thoughts in these essays are musings on the state of digital rhetoric and emphatically not a companion to the thought of Heidegger, but this characterisation of a purblind view of the truth seen through the prism of a technological frame of mind is a useful, albeit loose, conceptual framework in which to think about the internet and the ways we use it to communicate. Many of the conventions which govern the way we use the web reflect the world as *Bestand*. We have taken to the internet because it allows us to do all manner of things more efficiently: shop, meet people, be entertained, pay tax, vote. But just as thinking about the river solely as a source of energy misses something about the nature of rivers, so we lose something in the hyperreality of things which suit our convenience. These "painted flourishes", however appealing and pragmatic, do not win the heart of our French princess!

Consider cheesecake. If you buy cheesecake from the supermarket, you might read the mandatory notices about the volume of sugar and fat it contains, but most likely you won't. If, on the other hand, you make your own cheesecake, you will begin to appreciate how much sugar and fat goes into the stuff you blissfully fork down your throat. Perhaps you will even see it in a different light? If you aren't much of a cook and you don't have much time, then supermarkets are a convenience which will allow you to get your cheesecake without going to much bother. The internet, as in so many areas, has often just followed this through to a more extreme degree. These days, if I fancy some cheesecake, I barely have to move! I just visit a site – something like www.getcheesecake.com – click a few buttons and at some point in the not too distant future, cheesecake arrives at my door. Isn't it wonderful? In all of this, I don't need to know anything about how the cheesecake is made, the practices at the company which provides it, or anything about the poor minion paid a pittance to bike through a tempest at three in the morning just so I can contribute to rising levels of obesity. The internet has connected me easily to something I want, and yet, in a sense, I couldn't be more *disconnected* from reality.

This ultimately paints a very melancholy and bleak view of modern life: we are increasingly alienated individuals defined solely by our capacity to make elaborate calculations in our own interest (which, circuitously, only reinforce our state of alienation). And this seems to me to be in many ways true. There *is* something desperately sad and disenchanting about modern life, which the internet has only made worse.

Heidegger's glimmer of hope is our capacity to recognise the problem; or our capacity to think in a different way, to at once "enframe" the truth in a different way and recognise, as he puts it, that all truth is to some degree untruth, and so, mysterious. Where, I think, the internet bears out this glimmer of hope is in the stumbling and hypocritical practice of the "user experience" and "content strategy". These are, so to speak, the first thoughts, however infected and pock-ridden, beyond the univocal characterisation of things that the technological mindset entails. The user experience and content strategy show, under something like laboratory conditions, that people positively *want* more than a set of instrumental choices; they want personality, humour, art, colour, texture, things of real substance.

The most inventive and successful tech companies – as the story of *Apple* shows – are not the ones who invent new technologies, but the ones who make it work for human beings *as* human beings. In other words they are companies who see that there is more to a river than a source of energy. This means that the mood and momentum of digital rhetoric is peculiarly idealistic, and quite new juxtaposed with the unscrupulous reputation of advertising, communications and marketing. The internet, by probing the interests and sensibilities of people in more far-reaching ways, wants to "enframe" things in a more sensitive and nuanced fashion.

An idea which seems to say something very similar to the notion of "enframing" is "mediation". Truth must always be mediated through particular circumstances, shaped, moulded, creatively expressed through an unpredictable alignment of rare conditions. At its most sprightly and chipper, the forward gaze of communication online is towards a way of doing things which is looking for this rarity in order to celebrate it. The glint in the eye of digital rhetoric is similar to the search for the delicate details to which an artist's eye might attend.

By championing this line of thought, it would be a noisy contradiction and act of hypocrisy to offer these reflections as anything other than mediated through my own circumstances. They are not a systematically work- ed out enterprise of thought informed by exhaustive and penetrating research. They are academically ragged, as anyone who knows how to look will see easily. Instead they begin at the sharp end of trying to communicate – not always successfully – using the be- wildering range of digital tools now available. For the last eight years I have managed online communications at a national government agency, an experience which, for more than one reason, can induce light-headedness. So if the thoughts I have set out give the impression of vertigo, this might be why. It also means they are based on a heady cocktail of workaday interest, and moments of sheer panic at how to make sense out of an area of rapidly changing professional practice.

So I am not the chairman of Google or the CEO of a plucky and streamlined new startup in Shoreditch (though I do have a beard). I am an editor, trying to empathise with the cheerful ignorance of a lay perspective. And, through these eyes, I continue to think that digital communication is a land of plenty, however blighted by our failure to completely see and discover it.

Costard suffers for the King's ridiculous laws. The underlying thought here is, in a sense, that we suffer for a mindset that is every bit as ridiculous. And, to muddle my analogies, the further thought is that homemade cheesecake, when it turns out well, generally tastes better.

A new rhetoric: essays on using the internet to communicate

1.

Power struggles in the kingdom of content

A new rhetoric: essays on using the internet to communicate

When Bill Gates told the world that "content is king" he coined a cliché with which to repeatedly batter other vested interests in the hierarchies of digital technology. Websites might look pretty, they might even contain a lot of information, but if no-one wants to use the word "quality" about their content, then their overall quality will decline. Or so it goes.

All content needs a means or an instrument of some kind. A simple example might be speech. Words and thoughts are the content or substance of speech. The voice brokers these words and thoughts into being: the activity of the lungs, the larynx and the mouth. The means, where we can't restrain the urge to speak, is very much taken for granted, if not considered at all. But this should not disguise its relative complexity, sophistication and elegance.

We could say that speech might be considered a paragon of the form good communication should take: a body seamlessly, with no self-consciousness, delivers substance in a way that other bodies broadly understand. The noun is clearly the noun, and the verb is clearly the verb.

The printed word

At this relatively late stage in the history of printing and the printing press, there is noticeably less fascination with the technology that delivers printed words into our hands. Most readers are unlikely to pause in their perusal of some prose to marvel at the technology that made their activity possible. Most readers are interested in the content of the book, or newspaper, or magazine they are reading. Most readers, either consciously or unconsciously, assign the technology the logical status of "magic" and focus on the content it delivers to them.

If speech is a model for the form of good communication, then this means that the humble book, and the apparently superannuated printing press, are doing their jobs well. The means of production has not overlapped, interfered with, or otherwise trespassed on, the territory of its content. It has, in servile fashion, channelled data, thoughts, ideas, words, stories and so on, into the hands, hearts and minds of readers, without unnecessary self-disclosure or fuss of any kind.

This shouldn't fancy-dress the fact that the printing press was not born quite so effortlessly; and its role, importance, character and potential was not lost on either the forward- or backward-looking of the fifteenth and sixteenth centuries. Neither is it lost on historians. The "voice", under these circumstances, becomes the subject of many different enquiries, some purely empirical and scientific, others transparently commercial, and still others hotly, even dangerously, political and ideological.

Probably the most common example of the early printing press's preoccupation with itself was the sometimes over-inflated claims it liked to make, mainly for commercial reasons. In the largely monastic world of scribes and rubricators, scribal colophons came at the end of manuscripts. With the advent of the Gutenberg press, print workshops, alive to the need for promotion and publicity in order to cover their debt, put themselves at the front of their books, either in word or image. They also issued book lists and broadsides to raise awareness and expand their territory. So an integral part of the printing press' success as an innovation was its ability to draw attention to itself.

But self-promotion did not make the printing press a subject of controversy and historical curiosity. Its effects captured the attention of contemporaries and continue to fascinate historians. Put simply, as a piece of technology it made things possible that were previously not possible; and in doing so, it brought about tumultuous changes. It provided readers with access to material that they had not previously seen in ways they had not previously seen it. It expanded the volume of content or raw data available, and provided a means of distribution, quality control and standard-isation that allowed European culture to broaden its mind.

So the press brought about change; the kind of change it brought about was controversial; this there-fore raised awareness of the technology itself and made it a subject of controversy (and, of course, historical interest). Not surprisingly, the areas that saw the most controversial change were in the field of ideas and politics.

Historians might not agree about the extent of the press's influence, but it is more or less inconceivable not to consider it in an account of the Renaissance, the Reformation, or the Enlightenment. So, for those either agitating for change, or those anxious about change, or even for those looking back retrospectively to study all the forms of change, the technology, rather than perform its role as a seamless and unobtrusive channel for content, becomes a subject of calculations, analysis, intrigues, manipulation or political control.

The historian of the Reformation A G Dickens argues that Luther was "from the first the child of the printed book," so much so that Luther referred to the press in providential terms as a gift from God designed to free the gospels from the ignorance of the established church. Given the widespread influence that the press allowed Luther and other protestant reformers to exercise, this perspective was hardly surprising. And as Europe divided along theological and national lines, the different factions were quick to realise its importance. Just as Luther recognised and exploited the new technology, so did the Catholic Church after the Council of Trent, from which period the imprimatur and the index of prohibited books dates.

This provides an example of technology triumphing over content in a slightly different way. The political circumstances of the Reformation meant that an acute awareness of the technology and its power affected, or restricted, what could be said through it. Because the religious groups recognised its power, they exploited it for rhetorical and political purposes, limiting the nature of the content, in some cases to a comparatively narrow, proselytising purpose.

So, in the early days of the printing press, the *press as technology* was a subject of scrutiny because it was new and trying to advertise its potential, because it, often controversially, provided a way to change the nature and terms of debate and culture, and because it was quite simply an innovation that made all sorts of new things possible.

Are our internal organs on display?

Like the printing press, the internet is more than just a technological innovation. It too provides a way of mining for data at deeper levels and on a scale previously unimaginable. It too has already changed the ways human beings go about their lives and certain aspects of modern culture.

Like the early days – or decades, if not centuries – of the printing press, the web itself and its myriad technologies have managed to capture a lot of attention. This attention is a limpet on the back of the new possibilities which abound. In fact the attention is now more like a great swollen leech, that almost draws attention *away* from its possibilities. The interest in the new technology also bathes those who know how to wield it in a more glamorous light. These sexed-up scientists – the celebrated nerds and geeks of the last few years – have become a recognisable species with their own aesthetic.

Importantly, the attention fixed on the technology has made it a means and an end in itself. A large number of blog posts are about blogging or whatever the latest development or technological trend might be, just as a high proportion of tweets and wikis have technical content. This is hardly surprising since technologically minded people are most likely to understand, and be familiar with, the way the technology can be used, and so will use it to talk *about* their work. Still, it swings arms with more than a hint of something professionally narcissistic, as though a new technology carries with it an invitation to reflect on it, and write about it, and in doing so this justifies or consolidates the purpose of the technology.

A permanent search for innovation or the latest big idea is a related trend, which carries with it a more disparaging attitude towards slightly more dated inventions. This "fashionista", or perhaps even "teenager", view of technology is partly spurred on by the pot of gold that lies at the end of any successful invention, but also by technology as a cultural accessory. Whether it is a new gadget (from *iPod* to *blackberry* to *iPhone*) or a website (from *Napster*, to *MySpace* to *Facebook* to *Instagram*) its "newness" is almost as important as what the technology actually does. So a new bit of kit or a new "means" supersedes the content, data, substance or "end" it is designed to serve.

In both the case of technologists using new technology to talk about new technology, and the fetishization of the latest trends in technology, the idea of substance is, if not lost altogether, then substantially diminished. To return to the image of the human voice, it is as though we have become preoccupied with slitting open the throat and staring at the larynx, rather than just letting it do its job. The "verb" has become the "verb" *and* the "noun", but surely at the expense of grammatical coherence?

Creating "personas" is one of the common practices among those who try to make technology accessible for the user. These are representations of related user behaviour distilled into the characteristics of an imaginary person. And in the prevailing world of geeks and over-excited teenagers, or teenagers and over-excited geeks, it is sometimes possible to spy a fringe persona, but one that might just represent the majority.

This persona is a little more "middle of the road". Perhaps they are professionals with a penurious ration of time. Perhaps they are young parents who, while vaguely aware of the internet, have never really got to grips with it, and certainly haven't had the time to discriminate between a mashup and something you eat with sausages and gravy. This persona is time-con-sumed, always on the point of exhaustion, sensing older age, and a slightly ashamed Radio 2 listener. Not that they don't want to use the technology; they just don't want to have to study it or obsess over it. Technology which allows you to book a holiday more easily or watch a film is fine, this persona says. In fact it's something they might even mutedly applaud, as long as it doesn't break easily and is no more challenging than a Mr Men book.

Considered from this perspective, the social networking site *Twitter* has an interesting history. Like many online innovations, when it first came out there was a fair bit of excitement around it. Geeks and young people got interested. People of a certain generation scowled. Then the people at the cutting edge started to lose interest and get bored or started thinking of it as a bit passé, at which point the world's radio 2 listeners suddenly got interested. Twitter and tweeting has been on the rise ever since.

This brief history is a significant development in the wider kingdom of content, because it shows that technologies become most important when they are adopted by the people who care least about them. Or, to express this differently, they become most important when they are put to human rather than technical use.

In the last ten years or so, as the blind perfidy of human intelligence recognises that there is something useful about the internet while remaining equally baffled by it, those who create websites have simply *had* to respond accordingly if they are to compete. The "user experience" is now such a fundamental part of web design and development that it has almost become its first premise.

Businesses and governments are, then, alive to the need to make their technologies and the content they serve available to the ordinary man and woman on the street. Important as this shift is – and it is a battle that is still very much being fought – making something pleasurable to use is not the same thing as content. Websites, books, experts exist, all of which will explain good practice for usable websites. It would be possible to take this good practice and build a usable website, which might even bring with it a fleeting frisson of pleasure, even if the site had only a bare minimum of content. A user might just about be able to find their way around the site seamlessly and have a pleasurable –

or at least satisfying – experience, even if they had no interest in the content.

So how far does that matter? Sticking with the same historical parallel, Martin Luther did not publish his *97 Theses* solely because he wanted to create something that his readers could seamlessly access and enjoy, but out of raw piety, or because he thought that what he was publishing was intrinsically valuable, right and true. Luther was a theologian eaten up with passion for the articles of faith in which he believed; and this passion and ideological spirit made his tracts powerful. The printing press, combined with the unique circumstances of early sixteenth century western Christendom, magnified this power and passion, precipitating much greater impact than his work otherwise would have had.

So the question of the "user experience" is an interesting part of the web's short history. The technology clearly came first. The user experience came second. It came second because human beings, fitfully, clumsily, with a sort of default incompetence, realised that the new tool has the potential to serve intrinsic interests, appetites and ideas, but also realised that they don't have the time, energy or aptitude to understand the technology in its unadulterated form. Usability and the user experience help us to overcome this obstacle. They also underline content as the thing that really matters, because they exist to make the content possible; they bring the new technology in touch with the data, or material which fires human interest.

To extrapolate a view in panorama, it's my impression that for all the pioneering work that user experience (or "UX") professionals are doing, there still remains a wide gap between the state of the technology and the way "ordinary" human beings make sense of it. Basic features of the web that are too easily taken for granted remain mysterious for large numbers of people. If this (unfounded) observation is accurate, then it means content is still a king in waiting, or a prince with only a tenuous claim to the title.

Given the sheer volume of data that the internet is now generating, it's interesting to speculate that once the "UX" question is answered (or even comes close to being answered), there is no telling what kind of conflagration the spark of human interest might ignite. And if it's anything like the violent upheavals of the Reformation, this might not be all good news …

The network behind the throne

The relationship of noun to verb, voice to body, or in other words "content" to "technology" considered so far is fairly static. The content will always remain the same content, irrespective of the technology, just as the technology remains uninfluenced by the content. The content is the "what" and the technology is the "how". When a voice says "My name is heretical" the statement will remain true whether or not the person has a voice with which to say it.

But are content and technology that discrete? Does the nature of the technology make no fundamental difference to the content? In a very obvious sense, anyone looking at a website and comparing it to a magazine will quickly realise that there are clear differences (despite any number of similarities). Like magazines and newspapers, the web is a combination of written and visual content. On the web, audio and video also complement the writing.

An often bemoaned characteristic of digital content is its fragmented and pithy nature. Studies into the way people read online show that they do so much slower, and tend to scan rather than read line by line. More or less all web writing guidance teaches authors to adopt an evangelical version of the inverted pyramid, keep sentences, paragraphs (pretty much everything) short, and not to use ponderous language.

The prevalence of the web, and the prevalence of this way of writing for it, now mean that this is also affecting the way in which people read *as such*. Research has already begun to expose a generation of readers who are unable to concentrate on texts for any length of time, and, are unable to interrogate and unpick the dense layers of meaning, ambiguity and interpretation they contain. Translated into an outlook on life, the world becomes more fast-paced, immediate, superficial, and fickle, (but, perhaps, clearer and more concise).

"A picture paints a thousand words" is another cliché . So perhaps what web users lose in economy they gain in greater visual impact. We may be diving to the same depths just in a different way; the nature of the technology has changed the nature of the content from a more text-based medium, to one that also leans heavily towards visual forms of communication. A "statement" on the web uses more than the grammar which governs prose, but relies as much on less formalised, and slightly more mysterious, visual semantics.

This is all very vague, and, as with so much about the web, there is a sense of exploring the unknown, with all the excitement, awe, not to mention anxiety and trepidation, this entails. But if the changes that the web is bringing about are in some sense comparable to the changes brought about by the printing press, then there is reason to think that these first signs of a change in behaviour should be taken seriously.

Neither should we underestimate their extent. The way people read, and the fallout this has for the way they think and behave, is a substantial change. Some historians even argue that the printing press as a technology changed our understanding of fundamental philosophical categories, like time and identity.

The medieval view of time, under even fleeting scrutiny, does not offer the sort of hard, mechanical rigour we have come to expect in the modern world. It can seem a little slapdash, and prone to break down entirely through the eyes of saints and mystics in their riveting disruptions of the sublunary world. Bells ring out at each hour of the day, but the bell does not have the consistency of a mechanism, and with these human foibles – perhaps the bell-ringer has been known to get drunk – we might lose a few minutes here or there. Time is, in any case, just an imperfect reflection of eternity.

In a similar way, the modern essay is seen as a product of the printing press and is usually traced back to Montaigne. Montaigne created a distinctive literary genre because he chronicled, in a candid and intimate way, his private or personal life. Private and personal experiences were nothing new, but it was new to write about them publicly. This more informal style and means of writing, created in the public mind the notion of private space in which a private "self", or personal identity, could flourish. The proliferation of books and reading reinforced this sense of private identity; where previously most popular forms of communication were public and social, the printed book made possible the notion of withdrawing to a world of internal thoughts.

If the introduction of a technological revolution is capable of transforming metaphysical categories like time and self, what potential might lie in the digital revolution?

Prognostications - or in the jargon "futurism" - in the face of questions like this are usually shown to be wrong. But why let that get in the way of some sketchy speculation?

Transcendence

One of the things that the changes in perceptions of time and identity have in common is a broader and characteristically modern shift towards "objectivity". To think about - and measure - the world at a distance creates a tripartite distinction between observer, means and object of observation. This begins to lay the foundations for a stable, determinate, categorical and discrete view of the world. In the same fashion, the idea of a "private self" reinforces the notion of a situated position from which to look, ironically and dispassionately, at the cut and thrust of things.

Large leap as it might be, but characterised in this way, the broad outline of something like Cartesian dualism begins to take shape. Two incommensurate realms form part of the way in which to describe reality: the mind and the body. The mind stands securely in its peerless observatory mapping out the shifting firmament of the body and the material world. One way to read the Cartesian cogito in context might even be as a philosophical articulation of, or reduction from, these kind of category changes.

A striking point about both the printing press and the web, is that they have unleashed large volumes of information or data which were previously not available (or at least not as widely and easily available). In the case of the printing press, those who took advantage of it, rode the wave of information with a kind of buoyant confidence. Suddenly the flood of information and knowledge made the wider world considerably more intelligible, controllable and predictable. Human beings, armed with technology, such as precisely printed and standardised maps, could literally conquer the world.

The data that the internet has generated, and is generating, might be thought to only reinforce the trend established at the height of modernity. But the sheer volume of this data doesn't always bring with it the same sense of confidence; if anything, it is now almost overwhelming, exhausting and confounding.

To illustrate this simply, suppose I have some interest in marmalade. I might go to Google, and – without adopting a particularly discriminating approach – I might just type in the word "Marmalade". In 0.3 seconds I am confronted with over 18 million links to web pages around the world, that might (possibly) be relevant to my interest. 18 millions web pages (of whatever quality and relevance) goes way beyond my ability to assimilate them (even *just* for quality and relevance).

Google, acutely alive to the needs of those searching, doesn't simply match search terms to web pages. It will try to work out what your interests are and what content is relevant to you. It is already filtering the data, or accepting the extent to which the volume of data is transcending the ability of those with an interest in it to make sense of it. Information is the blood in the veins of the internet, but the most precious form of information has form: it is carefully selected for a specific purpose or need, and delivered in a digestible way.

There are some potential paradoxes here. The "objective" way of looking at the world broadly and loosely fostered in the course of the seventeenth and eighteenth centuries, turned on the notion of facts, figures, observations, and knowledge that were true independently of any given perspective. This way of seeing things became, for a cultural elite, *the* way to look at the world. The paradox is that the more information that is available, the less this way of looking at the world seems feasible, and the more knowledge can only ever be useful, purposeful or meaningful from a particular perspective, or a clearly delimited point of view.

If all this has some ground to it, then surely it affects categories like time and identity (and quite possibly many other philosophical categories) in an equally paradoxical way. The "self" it illuminates is very different from the Cartesian cogito, but it is not a relativised chimera. Identity and time become conditions *particular* to human nature. Borne out by these changes, the transcending nature of the information age also gives a clearer hint about human nature, because it marks out its boundaries.

Ellipsis

Print publishing models conventionally involve some kind of hierarchy. Those who own the means of production also exercise quality control over what they produce, informed by the nature and aims of the publishing house. Authors, or content producers, must try to understand the print houses which are most relevant to their talent, and meet the standards (or impress the editors with control over them) in order to publish their material. This restricts what gets published.

The advent of the internet has already had a profound impact. Blogs, various social networking sites for authors, the ease with which it is possible to set up your own website, plus self-publishing facilities, all mean that authors can publish their work fairly easily. Whether anyone will take any notice is another matter, and its quality might easily be dubious, untrustworthy or simply poor. In fact it is a fairly safe bet to assume that *most* self-published material on the web is not particularly high quality.

So these changes have not, so far, emasculated publishers, but they do have the potential to change the manner of their business. Rather than browbeaten editors painfully sifting through the slush pile, or making judgements on the basis of a pithy speed read, they can use the self-selecting power of the web to steer their editorial judgement. Editors can use online "hype" as a way of narrowing down their choices, possibly with a view to considering those choices more carefully.

These sort of changes to the publishing industry might not, to an outsider's eye, look especially bold or revolutionary. And yet they could signify something much more far-reaching. The technology now makes it possible to give a public voice to those who did not previously have one. In the same way that online publishing has allowed unpublished authors to publish their material, so too, in a more abstract sense, societies and cultures might begin to "think thoughts" which had previously gone unnoticed. This could happen for no other reason than the technology gives different perspectives (possibly previously silenced or reticent perspectives) the chance to articulate. (In the world of the web it isn't *necessarily* the most strident who have pride of place.)

Academics are already quick to acknowledge difference as a condition of their research. It has almost become a subject of satire. Historians, social scientists, geographers, archaeologists, philosophers, students of literature, all approach their subjects through cultural niches, and new accounts and narratives unfold from the perspective of gender, sexual orientation, social class, and ethnic background (among others). Some of this often feels like it challenges power with more power. It is assertive, even aggressive, designed as much to subvert, satirise, challenge or topple the perspective of an especially thrusting and assertive demographic - the church, the political elite or a "male, pale, and stale" hegemony - with a spurious claim to one prevailing story. But it could be that, if conventional wisdom privileges the reflective gaze of one identity over another, that this is as much a problem institutionalised by the mores and modes of communication as a brutal skirmish on the part of a self-aggrandising and dup-licitous elite. The hierarchical model of publishing is, as we have already seen, necessarily privileged. To retell the story from a different perspective (or even a series of different perspectives) only shares the privileged office more equally without challenging the privilege itself.

The internet provides a new communications infrastructure that places almost no prior restraint on who can and cannot speak or write, or, in some other way, voice their perspective publicly. Its dissenters see this more as a problem than a bright new dawn, since it only leads to the daily dissemination of seemingly interminable inanity, or, at best, it drastically affects quality and standards. That may be true, but a field smeared with manure also fertilises new crop.

To draw a different analogy, the effusion of publishing creates an environment a bit like the Wild West in which a phalanx of rogue voices are all competing for attention and speculating on a glorious reward. Many dead-ends, hollow triumphs, bloody brawls, might occur, but out of them will begin to emerge new and vibrant pockets of civilisation. What exactly this reshaped content will look like is almost anyone's guess; but, critically, it will not acquiesce to a pre-defined structure, with the battle for representation and difference that this entails. The internet, more than traditional forms of content, assumes "difference" as a condition of identity, to a degree that we cannot sensibly imagine or predict. To privilege the voice of someone because of their gender or ethnicity shows a peculiar *insensitivity* to difference and, by this light, glimpses the paradox of illiberal liberalism.

The web not only empowers a broader range of content but also provides alternative ways to capture and express it: where the printing press relied heavily on the printed word, the web allows content to be expressed in ways that are written, visual, oral or a combination of all three. This means that those who think in more visual terms, or are happier talking rather than writing, can express themselves in their preferred idiom. Difference, here, is not just a condition of identity but of the ways - the vocabulary, style, grammar, custom - in which identities communicate.

What the web makes possible, if this is to be believed, is a Byzantine world of content built up organically from widely distributed differences and experiences. This would, undoubtedly, be a world of complexity, but one in which potential that may cur-rently pass unrealised – if not positively frustrated – can find life and expression.

But enfranchising the elliptical is more than just a cultural nicety. Its ultimate explanation leads back to something much more visceral, primitive and attention-grabbing: the nature of power.

Politics

These kind of changes, if at all probable, will not come about because a small cabal of individuals decide to let them happen. They will come about because the technology empowers people in new ways, giving them the freedom to *participate* or have a much more active stake in the world that is immediately around them.

In the world of publishing, the internet has the potential to channel new voices and so challenge a monocentric imbalance in the public zeitgeist. In the world of politics the internet has the potential to give power to a broader range of people, and challenge the concentration of power in a distant and distorted elite.

National newspapers straddle both these worlds neatly, and the problems they face of dwindling readership and circulation go to the heart of the matter. The widespread availability of rival forms of content on the web (which are very often available for free) is a direct challenge to traditional newspaper reporting. Different sources of information inevitably bring with them a similar polyphony of opinions. Where the national newspapers might be relied upon to reinforce the opinion or perspective of particular readerships, the broadening range of online content can quickly undercut these stalwart but stubbornly entrenched positions.

The primary political colours of the national press could easily begin to look like a clumsy caricature of a more complex and diverse reality. *The Daily Telegraph* versus *The Guardian,* or to think it through differently, The Broadsheets versus The Tabloids, become crude simplifications that are no longer in tune with the way in which different readers or consumers of information in society think about, and make sense of, public life.

So the journalist's problem looks a lot like the web browser's problem and the publishing house's problem. Their own judgement might look pitifully inadequate and submerged next to a rising ocean of information and perspective, but perhaps they need to find new ways to become better informed by this information, rather than stand aloof from it. Journalism of this sort might become more responsive to the reflex movements of society, rather than operating inside inflexible ideologies and contracted public personas.

The skills of journalism would shift with the movements of the time. The credibility and authority of information, much of which will be wholly incredible and specious, places a premium on the ability to recognise valuable material. So even if journalists aren't first at the scene and crafting the story into a knockout blow, they will have the skills to know a good source from a bad one and curate what the reading public should (and should not) give credence.

The metropolitan world of the media is, however, almost a by-product of the world on which it is, for the most part, reporting: the world of corporate business and particularly corporate government. In modern democracies, governments are clumsy, clunking instruments that squat uncomfortably on the body politic. Conventionally they empower their citizens through the notion of "choice". The electorate does not make decisions about public administration directly; it votes for a small body of people with shared views about public policy to make the decisions on their behalf or to act as their representatives. But the *exercise* of government remains the privilege of an elected few.

Clustering around this elected few are an equally small number of journalists. Both groups, under the current arrangements, exercise extraordinary power. In the same way that political decision-making is con-densed into the narrow political space of an executive power, so too the way it is understood by the electorate is condensed into the same primary political colours that inform the editorial judgement of newspapers. The complex details of public policy are honed down into pithy sound bites, and three-minute heated exchanges on *Newsnight*. This inevitably means that politics is reduced to a kind of lubberly partisanship, because that is the only way members of the public can identify it at all within the time and space available. Politics, political parties and the way this is reported and haphazardly controlled through the media, become tribal encampments of ideology that move with the dexterity and intellectual agility of a sloth.

Anyone who even scratches the detail behind any given policy initiative of any given government in a modern democracy will quickly spot the incongruity between the fine-grained, technical detail and the way in which it is presented to, and "understood" (though mostly misunderstood or ignored) by, the public. This incongruity entails the *nature* of modern government, regardless of political ideology or party political loyalty, precisely because power, even in enfranchised societies, is concentrated in such a small space.

This seems to stand in marked contrast with the potential that internet technologies can harness. The web, as we have seen, has the power to channel new voices, and directly empower their opinions, concerns, agendas or even simply their observations of the world around them. By nurturing greater variety, unless we assume that established categories of thought already exhaust our ability to make sense of political reality, we might begin to discern a deeper, broader, fuller picture of that reality against which the pendulum of social democracy and laissez faire neoliberalism, or the "Labour versus Tory" view of things, looks crude and simplistic.

If the public, or a group within the public, feel strongly enough about a local issue, it is within their power to gain access to detailed information about the issue, and even have a direct conversation with those who are responsible for it. In a more proactive sense, the communications infrastructure that the web and its associated technologies provide, allow relatively small groups to organise themselves and agitate on a particular subject matter in ways that were not previously possible. At present only those who under-stand the technology well enough might find the mot-ivation, but if this kind of behaviour were to become perilously normal, then an individual could end up involved in a range of views on a range of topics, that are broadly inconsistent with a party line, and imp-ossible to "rationalise" *into* a party line. The grand ideological view of politics would become nothing more than a simplified caricature of a much more complex society, acting, evolving and behaving in possibly very different ways.

So perhaps the political content of many modern newspapers looks caricatured because it is simply an accurate reflection of the world - or village - on which it reports. The broadcast portrait of national politics looks like a caricature, because national politics is a caricature of the reality that sits distantly, looking empty-headed and unwashed, behind it. National pol-itics isn't "political science"; it's an especially hammy form of theatre (very often with wooden actors).

In a practical sense, technology is already shedding light on the secrets of government, or the idea of a metropolitan elite at the centre of things, and making it possible to build up centres of power locally. The work of almost all government organisations (in the UK anyway) is now available online, and the UK government is addressing how this information might meet the needs of those that have an interest in it. This fact alone is intriguing, and there is a curious and

interesting challenge for all those involved professionally in its publication. Is the information that
corporate government publishes simply dry technical
detail of interest only to specialists, or can it be a rival to
the kind of content that has traditionally been (and for
the moment continues to be) available in national
newspapers?

Accountability through greater transparency is a
hot topic, but the full extent of transparency might
entail meaningful and objective conversations directly
with the public (or relevant interest groups) about
government activity, in a way that the more flavoured
political rhetoric of newspapers cannot provide. A free
press has always been seen as essential in free societies
in order to hold governments to account, but a
transparent and publicly controlled (or even publicly
owned) government might make government
accountable in more direct, powerful and meaningful
ways.

Cynics might give a hollow laugh at this point.
The idea that any government would engage in
objective and meaningful conversations through
communications channels that it controls might be seen
as something misty-eyed and ridiculous. Similarly the
idea that a relatively ignorant public could realistically
engage with government on matters of complex public
policy might seem equally deluded.

And yet "cynicism" itself falls under the swoop
of this thought's eagle flight. One way to explain this
kind of cynicism is as a product of political disen-
franchisement, an unwanted product which a technology like the web has the potential to help remedy.

Cynicism presupposes a centralised government in an entrenched, agenda-driven position seeking to bias the way its own activity is understood by the public (which might be described differently as "propaganda").

It also assumes that the public has "contracted" the business of government to politicians, and the experts who serve them, leaving the public in a passive, but judgemental, role. Under these arrangements, how is it possible that the public could be perceived as anything other than relatively ignorant? Surely the social contract is designed to allow for this, and in allowing for it, legitimises and almost provokes it?

Some level of cynicism in this unequal distribution of power must be inevitable. The *condition* of a government so-constituted must produce a degree of cynicism because (even if it is well-intentioned) it will, by definition, not speak for all constituencies of the body politic, leaving those disenfranchised, cynical about its activities.

In any televised debate between politicians and the public, the public almost always assumes (by default) a cynical attitude towards the politicians in general and the incumbent administration in particular, regardless of their political colours. This suggests, paradoxically, that the voice of the public, even carried by the electoral register, thinks of itself as partly alienated from the exercise of power, and therefore either angry, disillusioned or perhaps simply indifferent.

It's almost a simple arithmetical argument to suggest that the internet might help this predicament. If a technology brings more people into the picture of public affairs, then it begins to dissolve some of (or even a large part of) the difference between "the public" and "government". If democracy means power by the people, then the streak of cynicism which underpins most public debate implies a farce: that people are cynical about their own judgements.

Alternatively, we are less "democratic" than we like to think. But a stronger territorial claim to the business of government among the public, might over-come the prevailing attitude of anger, disillusionment and cynicism. It would no longer become meaningful to talk and think of "the government" as somehow a separate entity from the instincts and judgement ("good" and "bad") of society. The dualistic and dis-membered "them and us" world of modern gov-ernment would become a *genuine* body politic with a complete range of fully functional limbs.

Rather than an elected sovereign, or a small coterie of individuals chosen to exercise considerable power at the head of government, the sprawling, unpredictable and constantly evolving nature of civil society might take more direct ownership of the institutions of government, to create a diverse political culture in a complex political space. The Hobbesian Leviathan would crumble on its own insecure foundations.

Ends and means

These fairly wild speculations about the future, and the moderately more grounded examinations of the past, suggest that technology is at its most mercurial and significant when it serves something of substance. It finds a role and purpose, and has the potential to bring about powerful and dramatic changes, when it is yoked to particular objectives, insights, and ambitions. It is, in short, at its most provocative and intriguing when it mimics the human body: when it becomes the "voice" with which to articulate something that would otherwise remain abstract and without form.

This conclusion comes with a qualification; by giving form to an abstraction, technology by definition also limits, and to some extent conditions, the nature of what would otherwise remain "pure thought". Technology affects the form its content takes; or to put it in broader terms, the nature of the "means" influences the nature of the "end". When a person articulates a thought, or – as now – when they write it down, the physical act of articulating gives it a form that is particular to the act. In the same way, when the web is used to publish content, the content adapts to the nature of the technology. The suggestion here has been that the web, as a particularly flexible technology, has the potential to produce a more variegated approach to content, or, relatively speaking, a less restricted approach that can more adequately represent the natural range of differences.

This qualification, therefore, suggests that, on the one hand, it is impossible to think the notion of "an end" without inferring a means; but also that the use of a means towards a particular end is only appropriate where the end it suited to the nature of the means. A handbag is not particularly useful as a communications tool, but the internet is. The ultimate and most basic end of a body might be described as "to live", since an inanimate body runs contrary to its nature. The range of ends that attend a body's broader aim "to live" would, then, need to consider the nature of a living body. Falling in love might be thought of as an end that is proper to the nature of a living body. But is something like the pursuit of wealth? Or acts of courage? Or acts of magnanimity?

What this suggests, quite apart from the broad debate over ethical behaviour that it opens up, is that proper ends have a value that is intrinsic to the nature of the context in which they occur. A body has a range of proper ends. A voice has a proper end: to articulate. In the same way the nature of any technology (such as the web and the printing press) will have a proper end, or a complex range of proper ends intrinsic to its nature. What something as simple and real as a body or a voice shows something as apparently complex as the web, is that all means fulfil their proper role when they serve ends that are inherent. The kingdom of content on the web only truly reigns when the means (the technology) serves the end (the content), when both ends and means dovetail in a kind of perfect harmony.

The interdependence of ends and means (that is governed by the nature of the means) might be taken to imply that all ends are *relative* to their means. An end cannot be meaningfully transposed from one context to another without invoking an equivalence that would not appear to exist. The form that web content will take is necessarily different from the form of the printed word because the nature of the technology is fundamentally different. While it may be possible to say similar things – even the same things – through the two idioms, the idiomatic difference will at some level affect the content.

It may be true to say that the difference between an end pursued through different means will inevitably affect the nature of the end, even if the difference is only nuanced, as in the case of the same piece of content published in print and online. But does that mean that an end has no meaning (explicit or implied) beyond the context that gives it form?

In the case of print and the web, if a publisher uses both to publish the same content, this content is the end for all the different forms it takes. In the case of a thought this might be articulated orally or in written form, through sign language or some other gesture; but the thought remains the same. The different means of communicating might suit or condition the thought in different ways (some, for example, leaving it more amb-iguous than others, or some more engaging than others), but all the different means flow from the same end.

This all suggests that ends are not, then, entirely relative to the means. There is, perhaps in an elliptical sense, something beyond the means. And this is as true for the life of a body as it is for a bit of content published in both a magazine and on a website.

2.
The web and the art of memory

Information, depending on how you look at it, can be both spectacular and a consecrated pain in the backside. This applies particularly in the case of the web. An entire universe of information has emerged with its growth. It's almost exhausting even to think about trying to make sense of it, so much so that "making sense of it" is now every bit as important as the information itself. The web is, in other words, partly heuristic – it is about organising the information it has joined up. Staring fixedly (and perhaps a little forlornly) at this goal, it is still stumbling successively through re-inventions of the filing cabinet.

What might seem, at first glance, particular to the web is also more widely on display. Commentators on the state of modern working life very often draw attention to how the amount of information is overwhelming everyone and how little time they have to assimilate it. Entrepreneurs on the scent of a kill are, if anything, even more incisive. The marketing pitch for an indeterminately large number of software products focuses on this particular problem, conveniently glossing over the fact that it also contributes to it (as we all do …).

The web

Even within the comparatively narrow domain of a single website, web designers and content editors still sweat over how to arrange and organise the information in the easiest and most accessible way. There are now a range of different ways in which web developers and software giants have responded to this problem. Search has, for a long time, been a fundamental part of the solution. Organising information into tree-like hierarchies or categories, navigable or filterable in different ways, is another convention.

An intriguing, and perhaps still inchoate, part of this side to the web, is the role of design. The comparatively new area of the "user experience" draws attention to the importance emotional response has for the ease and willingness with which users will embrace a site. Design is fundamental to this response, and many modern sites, will expend more energy on making their sites "look good" or "awesome" with this philosophy in mind. It is also acknowledged that intelligent visual design can affect the way users interact with a site; how a specific bit of functionality – a button, a menu, a search box etc – looks may affect how much, or how easily, it gets used.

But the extent to which design plays a part in organising and structuring the information is, currently, largely confined to simple ways in which content is laid out on a page: in columns, rows, widgets, boxes and so on. And yet the idea that design, or at least the use of imagery, should be more central to this is not by any means new, and has a long, if ironically forgotten, heritage.

The art of memory

The art of memory begins with the ancient Greek poet, Simonides. Simonides, the story goes, was attending a banquet at Thessaly held by a nobleman, Scopas. Scopas had contracted Simonides to compose for him an honorific poem, but Simonides, to the chagrin of his host, took the opportunity to include a eulogy for the gods, Castor and Pollux. In the course of the banquet, Simonides received a message that two young men were waiting for him outside. He withdrew outside but could not find the two young men. In this time, the roof of the banquet hall collapsed and crushed all those inside beyond recognition, so much so that the relatives of those deceased could not identify them. But Simonides found that he could do so because he could remember where they were sitting.

This story provides the essential insight behind the art: Simonides could identify the crushed bodies because he could associate them with a place or order in his recollected mental image of the banquet hall. The art turns on the organising power of an arresting image to bring structure to information.

The life-support machine for anyone who is trying to work their way back through the original sources to this story is Frances Yates' now classic history of the subject. As Yates tells us, Simonides' story is not recorded in any existing Greek text. The earliest available texts that mention the art prominently are three Latin sources on the subject of rhetoric: Cicero's *De Oratore*, Quintilian's *Institutio Oratoria*, and a work of anonymous authorship, the *Ad Herennium*. The Roman world knew about the art as a technique that public orators and logicians could master for the practical purpose of persuasion. These texts boast that those who have mastered it develop the capacity to absorb large volumes of information in a structured and skilful way.

The classical rhetorician's study of the art takes a textbook-like form, and, despite nuances, follows the same broad approach: the object of the memory must be made to conform to a structure or an order of some kind using a context or background, and images should be used to make items within that structure memorable. Crucially, the images must be striking in some way or another: whether they are especially beautiful, ugly, horrific or simply appropriate to the nature of the thing committed to memory. The "art" or "artfulness" of the images is, as such, a key part of the role they play in creating a memorable order.

Stated abstractly like this, it can seem that the classical exponents of the art almost had in mind something that was widely known but which has become lost. Quintilian rescues anyone looking for more context by putting a little more flesh on the bones. The student of the art, he writes, must choose a place, such as a spacious house with many rooms. They must first commit the layout of the house to memory, and then use memorable signs or representative symbols positioned in key parts of each room to recall the objects of their memory. The context of the location need not be a house or anything real; it can be a public building, the stages of a journey, a picture, or something imaginary.

The schooling that the art provides, according to the classical texts, gives the orator a means of mastering their information in a formidable and systematic way so that they are armed in order to be able to debate. The use of images, – or the "imagination" – under mentoring of this kind, has a very clear, focused and pivotal purpose.

From the classical world, as Frances Yates chronicles, the art was taken up by different traditions. Its shape and direction in the middle ages stays closest to the rhetorical purposes of the classical world, but adapted to a spiritual and devotional end. For both the classical speaker and the medieval believer, the art helps to address a question of transcendence: it helps the ancient orator to master volumes of information that go beyond ordinary powers of recollection; for the medieval believer, it forms part of the way in which human beings fulfil a natural orientation towards a transcendent God.

Thomas Aquinas gives the art its definitive medieval interpretation. He discusses it as part of a broader discussion about "prudence" or "practical wisdom". This term, with its origins in the Greek word "Phronesis" and Aristotle's Ethics, is described as a virtue particular to the nature of man and his rational capabilities. Aquinas, like his classical forebears, recognises memory as a component of prudence, along with intelligence and providence. If employed sensibly – or "artfully" – these three parts of a prudent soul, allow human beings to discern things that are "subtle and spiritual" in a way that is appropriate to the limitations of their nature.

Intelligence, for Aquinas, is the "part" of human nature that naturally intuits the "subtle and spiritual" things. The innate constraints on human nature mean that human intelligence cannot grasp intelligible things without forming a mental picture of them. This picture is the product of the imagination, which relies on sensory impressions from the external world. The rational part of the human soul that is drawn towards mind-bending pure abstractions, ultimately cannot exist without the art of imagination, which derives from a bodily existence.

This turns images and the imagination into a means suited to the nature of human beings that allows them to contemplate deeper, and transcending, spiritual and metaphysical truths. "Memory" here is not the recollection of legal cases, circumstantial details and technocratic rubric, but the recollection of abstract, almost elliptical and intimated intangibles, a broader spiritual "meaning" that impossibly resists and subverts meaning.

Perhaps because the goal is more exalted, Aquinas' discussion of memory as an art introduces some important conceptual changes. The images or symbols used to represent the object of recollection are no longer simply distinctive, but are described as "corporeal similitudes"; in other words, images "borrowed" from the material world to represent truths of intrinsic importance. Practitioners of the art should also, he enjoins, contemplate the images "with solicitude" and "cleave with affection" to them.

This more emotional language makes sense within a devotional tradition in which the ultimate object of devotion is intrinsically desirable. It suggests a use which is designed explicitly to call upon sentience or a range of emotions to direct and incite the student of the art towards their object of recollection.

This appears to be tacit in the textbooks of the ancient world; here authors of the art recommend the use of images that are especially striking, since the memory is more likely to retain those images that "stand out". Aquinas develops this aspect of the art in a way that is sometimes called "relational". For Aquinas, contemplation of God is, in the same motion, rational and affective: the more the believer contemplates God rationally, the more they discern God's love and vice versa. If love and understanding are entwined and human beings are reliant on images from the material world for their cryptic understanding of the more rarefied "spiritual" world, it follows that the images borrowed from the material world should also encourage devotion. Contemplation "with solicitude" is natural to the act of any proper spiritual contemplation.

The same relational logic means that the more truly desirable the object of contemplation, the more memorable (and so intelligible) it will become. Desire, knowledge and the attenuated roots of existence in its most abstract and overbearing sense, coalesce to an unthinkable degree. To disaggregate the technicalities of the art of memory (anachronistically) from metaphysics and theology, this at root means that Aquinas has developed a system in which the art has more effect when it also has strong emotional content.

The web and the art of memory

Following the art of memory only up to this point, it is possible to see how it might relate to something like the web, in spite of its classical heritage. The art might, at first glance, seem like a more elaborate version of a party trick: impressive, perhaps, but in the towering shadow of modern data and its associated technologies, a little quaint.

At root, though, it would seem that the art of memory and the web are concerned with something, if not exactly the same, then very similar: the use of information. It is a little restrictive to say that the internet is solely about joining up bits of information, but this is surely one intrinsic and cardinal part of its nature. The art of memory, in its classical form, aims to help public debaters assimilate extensive material for debating purposes. The web provides access to more information from across the world – often in real time – for anyone with a connection. Both are winning formulas, or technologies which consolidate a natural aptitude for managing and using more data.

Both not only provide access to the inform- ation, but also do so by creating an order or a structure of some kind. The web creates clusters of information – or "sites" – organised around a particular theme. Beyond this, search technology, all manner of faceted categorisation, as well as the mildly more recent self-organising wave of social media, all provide ways of breaking down, creating, re-structuring, sharing and customising the information the web contains in ever more particular and sophisticated ways.

The art of memory also creates order, but does so using a different technique: it harnesses the structure of art and imagery. The "logic" of an image does much the same thing as the complex mathematical logic of a search-engine algorithm, albeit in a more primitive, restrictive but perhaps more intuitive way.

This point is interesting. It might be possible to dismiss the art of memory with an amused wave of academic curiosity, as something antiquated and relatively simple. But the difference of technique between the art of memory and the collective methods of information-analysis and organisation on the web is more pertinent than it might at first seem.

The art of memory is clearly a human art, which finds its clearest expression in the analysis of Aquinas. By placing memory inside the broader virtue of prudence, Aquinas recognises it as a skill defined by human nature. The memory's use of images is natural, occurring intuitively and spontaneously, but, a little like, say, physical fitness, something that requires training and practice to develop or even perfect. The organising intelligence of the web is clearly not human; it relies on very clever, concatenated machines. But for companies and organisations charged with trying to organise the information, this is one of their big problems: the technology is so clever and technical that it becomes hard to use for most "ordinary" human beings.

Might then the art of memory, as a more intuitive tool for structuring information, provide a potential solution to the modern plight of online information overload? Many current practices in the area of web design appear to have almost pushed the web in this direction already. The subtleties of design on the web are well chronicled by endless manuals, sites and articles. Colour, font, imagery, layout and so on, all play a crucial part in the way users make sense of the online experience. The marrying of "sense" and "design" means that "web design" is already far more than just a purely aesthetic exercise. The aesthetics must serve the logic of user behaviour and psychology.

The recent emphasis placed on the "user experience", in a sense pioneered by people like Steve Jobs, also brings design into play in a different way. This philosophy recognises that human beings react to technology in thoroughly human ways. The way the technology is created elicits an emotional response, and the nature of this response may affect how easily they can use it, or how far they want to use it. Like Aquinas, the "UX" architect works on the assumption that there is an intimate – but innocent – relationship between a user's "desire" for something and how far they are likely to grasp it.

In prose it is sometimes said that an overarching metaphor or some form of figurative expression can help to crystallise an idea. Take a simple but very well-known example; in 1946 Churchill gave a speech at Westminster College, Missouri designed to galvanise a change of attitude towards the Soviet bloc of eastern European countries. Famously he said:

"From Stettin in the Baltic to Trieste in the Adriatic an iron curtain has descended across the continent."

From this point on, the "iron curtain" became a widely used and understood metaphor to describe the Soviet bloc, and an image emblematic of the cold war. As an image, it succinctly and evocatively captures the changing geopolitics of the time. The interesting, if only embryonic, ways in which the web uses design, and the clamour to make the web sexy, perhaps suggests that something like the use of Churchillian images might be used to bring together these trends. Or, to say it differently, one way to consolidate some of the practices designed to enhance the way the web communicates might be to use images in much the same way as the classical art of memory.

The use of "real world metaphors" is already an acknowledged and widely used practice for anyone involved in the practice of Human-Computer Int-eraction. It's only necessary to boot up "Windows" to realise as much. This practice takes the characteristics of something in the real world – a window – to help people use the operating system. The distinctive feat-ures of a window set the parameters for all the ways in which the data on the computer is presented. The same is true of files, folders, recycle bins, and desktops. All these images help ordinary users make sense of, and manage information through, the machine that sits before them.

Windows is probably one of the examples in the world of computing that comes closest to the classical art of memory since the image of a window actually is the environment in which all actions take place. The concept of "a window" becomes the key underlying concept for any ordinary user. Simple and easy to grasp as it might be, "a window" is not the most attention-grabbing and distinctive piece of imagery available to the senses! What is more, in the case of websites and many software packages, they rarely use images beyond this, except occasionally to make certain features or bits of functionality easier and clearer to understand.

To focus on the web, the design and layout of most websites, while it draws considerable attention, often turns on some very basic visual concepts: columns, rows and boxes. Very few sites use a uniquely memorable image as their organising principle. But, if there is anything at all to the art of memory, might this not mean that there is an unexplored opportunity here? Web designers have developed ever-more granular and smart uses for Cascading Style Sheets, the styling language used for controlling the presentation of HTML in a web browser. It does not seem incon-ceivable that these tools could be brought to bear on the mark-up, or the technical structure of the content on websites, or in web applications, to create graphical or visual experiences that have the dual purpose of organising information by effectively creating a work of art.

But as Churchill's celebrated turn of phrase suggests, perhaps an image need not always be so obviously visual. All images are, by their nature, visual, but Churchill takes tangible images and applies them to more abstract, diffuse and impersonal concepts. Where the examples just cited might require a lot of design and coding, all this takes is an act of imagination. The centre-right think tank *Respublica* has taken this approach; rather than call its blog a "blog" it has chosen a suitable metaphor to reflect its ideological position: "The Disraeli Room". This immediately conjures up an image of a physical location tucked away in some oak-panelled parliamentary estate where informal debates about public policy take place in a cloud of pipe smoke. It's memorable, appropriate to the content, and makes their site more personal and engaging, as well as creating clear expectations of the content.

Just like a Churchillian turn of phrase, imagery of this sort is unifying: it brings together the aims of organising the information and making that structure memorable with presenting it in an engaging and enticing way that is appropriate to the nature of the content. The ideal image, it might be imagined, is both a work of art in the sense that it inspires, excites and engages, but also a pragmatic instrument or tool geared towards a goal: in this case the discovery of inform-ation.

Art and communications

In the modern world the word "art" has certain connotations, and while these may not exclude the creation of objects or items that have a practical use, "art" is more often than not considered a refined and slightly aloof activity, admitted mainly to the realm of leisure, pleasure or exclusive insight. Paintings and art galleries, in the UK anyway, are for the most part places you visit in your spare time, for entertainment. The same can be said of fiction, poetry, film, music, games. Art, for its consumers, is not, for the most part, something practical or part of a workaday routine. It is not insinuated into the factory floor or the neurasthenic aridity of the office. These activities, for most people, are functional, practical, a sort of expedient offering at the altar of subsistence.

Granted purveyors of high culture will balk at the notion that Velasquez or Tolstoy should be considered merely entertainment. The fine arts might aim at loftier goals; they may even accept the idea that art should be valued for its own sake rather than as a pleasing distraction. But even this notion of aesthetic value is peculiarly removed from ordinary experience – or you might say, more simply, from life. Considered in this way high art can seem like the object of a masonic ritual inflated and distorted by secretive hearsay and lack of contact with ordinary human beings.

Weighed in the balance, the art of memory, on the other hand, and particularly any potential use it might have on something like the web, suggests that there is – speculatively and idealistically – a role for art that is more practical, immediate and rooted in particular experience. An image tendered to the art of memory has all the qualities of a work of art: it must be constructed and appreciated for its intrinsic merits; it must meet standards of excellence and distinction; it must excite a reaction, a feeling, an interest or an appetite of some kind. All the attributes that attract visitors to galleries, viewers to cinemas, readers to books, are qualities the art of memory adopts in the pursuit of its ends.

A painting by Velasquez is not an object set aside and considered purely in its own orbit of value. This is not to say that it has no intrinsic value, but rather that its intrinsic value derives from the purpose it is designed to illuminate. To take the example of Churchill's famous phrase, this is a finely constructed piece of language in its own right, but the full extent of its "artfulness" derives from the practical purpose and circumstances to which it relates.

This begins to suggest that the conveniently neat distinction between "high" and "low" art and culture is not quite as categorical as it might at first seem. It also begins to suggest that the world of work and the world of the imagination could perhaps learn a lot from each other.

Contracting works of high art to a practical purpose might for "high artists" seem a little too much like getting dirty hands, but if the implications of the art of memory are anything to go by, this suggests that these artists occupy a self-alienating bubble. Under the art of memory an artwork only really has value where its intrinsic merits serve some broader purpose. A painting with intrinsic merits would be superbly realised and speak directly to human nature and its rational and emotional sympathies, rather than a painting with the sole aim of selling Coca Cola or providing a bit of frivolous entertainment. But the quality intrinsic to the painting does not – and cannot – exist in isolation; the merit of the painting is joined at the hip with the object it is contrived to recall; and this provides the conditions or the environment in which the artwork must take shape.

There is a clear, and clearly important, distinction to attest here. An artwork that follows the art of memory recognises that whatever the result it must be something that has something like an "objective" value in itself, rather than a value that only comes from its success as an aide memoire. Yet the artwork cannot have an objective value without the aim or purpose it is there to fulfil.

The inverse of the kind of ideal that the art of memory appears to suggest fragments and distorts the artwork in different ways. Art for art's sake (art, that is, that has no stated purpose) is a little like a dismembered limb, or a cryogenically frozen head anticipating some sort of reanimation. To look at (or equivalently, to read, perform or watch) an artwork it might elicit a reaction; the substance might be there, but it is not directed at any end, and therefore its full resonance or value is partially, if not entirely, lost.

In the case of many medieval and renaissance paintings, this fragmentation is in many cases actually visible. Paintings that have been hacked and wrenched out of their place in the elaborate and colourful liturgies of the Christian (or equivalent) universe, hang on the walls of many museums a little like bloody body parts, with dried tissue and baked wounds.

"High art" conceived in this way, for all its pretensions to a more exalted value, begins to look empty, nihilistic and entirely self-regarding, as though it cannot contemplate a description of reality any bigger or broader than the dimensions of its own house and garden.

"Low art", to flip the coin, does something quite different. This kind of art, by definition has a firmly stated purpose, a goal at which it aims. Advertising aims to sell a product. Commercial fiction aims to sell copies. Big budget Hollywood movies aim to do well at the box office. Graphic designers, among other things, aim to build and maintain identifiable brands.

So-called "low art" does not suffer from the kind of brutalised fragmentation of art that stands aloof. But the danger, which applies as much to the art of memory as a practice, is that the end demeans the quality of the artwork. Or to put this differently, the danger is that the end at which the artwork aims intrudes upon its content in a way that makes it less interesting, engaging or desirable. The danger, in short, is that it turns sex into prostitution.

But surely organisations, just like people, have interests and are capable of expressing and exploring those interests in a way that entice people and organisations with similar interests. A supermarket should, in theory, have an interest in groceries, just as a government agency responsible for the natural environment should have an interest in the environment and its sustainability. The "problem" arises where the supermarket places its interest in a profit before its interest in its products, or where the government agency places its corporate reputation, or the politics that entails, before the welfare of the natural environment.

It might immediately be objected that a business that doesn't make a profit is a pretty poor business and not in a position to deliver a quality product, just as a government agency with a discredited reputation is not in a strong position to discharge its duty. But the issue is not an either/or, but one of priorities. The underlying assumption of the art of memory is that intrinsic interests serve practical ends better than artificial interests. A supermarket, in other words, that, within its means, values the product it is selling in itself is likely to do better business; just as a government agency that shows an intrinsic interest in its duties, is likely to elicit a better public reputation.

By the same logic, communications that simply "borrow" from popular culture (of whatever form) to champion their own narrow ends, are unlikely to be as successful as communications that are works of art in their own right.

The conclusion must be that whatever the stated aim – selling a product, recalling or organising some information, getting a corporate message across – "sex" works a lot better than "prostitution". The relationship of advertising and marketing to events which draw an intrinsic human interest is witness to this fact. The sponsorship deals that sporting events – such as the Olympics or high-profile football matches – enjoy shows that organisations looking to sell their product will pay handsomely to associate with something that people really value and which matters to them. The same might be said of the marketing and merchandising industry that clings like a limpet to movie blockbusters and franchises that popular culture embraces and loves. A simple illustration of this thought is the activity of an established charity who work to raise awareness of HIV in third-world countries, but who realised, in a moment of inspiration, that the best way to do this was in tandem with playing football.

This relationship between artwork and an aim or goal stops working, or begins to look tawdry, as soon as the intrinsic interest begins to look more like a superficial and instrumental interest. A question for an individual, or an organisation that wants to, in some way, use a piece of art (or an aspect of popular culture such as football) towards a goal, might then be does that individual or organisation have an intrinsic interest and appreciation of the art? The artist, in the same way, needs to be clear about why they are producing the piece of art. If it is just to sell a product or get a message across, then is it really art, and, just as importantly, is it really effective?

Underlying these observations is Aquinas' relational logic, the assumption of which is that the greater the draw or desire, the greater the understanding or appreciation, and vice versa. Within this logic a lack of imagination is fatal. A limited understanding of the world – which is surely the starting point for most people – can make things attractive that only appear to be attractive; and an attraction to things that are only superficially attractive reinforces a limited understanding of the world.

Organisations, businesses, advertisers, publishers and so on, maybe half-wise to this kind of thinking, but my sense is that they are only half-wise, and that this kind of lack of imagination is, in fact, largely the norm. Whether it is a business or a public sector body, a publisher or an advertising agency, all have a perverse incentive to understand "reality" on their own terms (in other words selfishly). This means that the kind of communications in which they engage – which they do at great financial cost and through a lot of spurious theorising – show very little sensitivity to how interesting the world really is. To draw a very real simile most "corporate communications" are like a caricatured narcissist lauding their own achievements. And most people react to these kind of communications as they would to this kind of character (that is, with little in the way of respect, and a lot in the way of cynicism).

By the same logic, communications that simply "borrow" from popular culture (of whatever form) to champion their own narrow ends, are unlikely to be as successful as communications that have a value in their own right. And, keeping within the same neighbourhood of thought, there should really be no need for the distinction between high and low art, as the values of "high" art should work within the aims of "low" art. Under these circumstances, artists would strike up conversations with businessmen to identify and communicate their common interests. But we live in the "real" world where artists talk to artists and businessmen speak the codified language of the water cooler.

It is worth stressing that this is not just a case of businesses becoming "tasteful" by extending their sponsorship or patronage to the production or creation of grand operas. The real challenge would be to sponsor the creation of a grand opera that articulates something that is essential to – and of interest to – the nature of the business. And the daunting final qualification to this line of argument is that this is really not an easy thing to do. In whatever circumstances, the creation of an opera, a novel, painting or film that strikes some kind of note within the resonant intervals of human nature, is an unpredictable and painstaking task. It is not risk free. If anything it has the character of a frightened leap in the dark. But if the art of memory is correct, the return ought to make even the most sleek and successful advertising campaign look grubby.

What's so special about the web?

Considered against this, crudely contentious, view of the relationship between art and communications, the web might look like just the latest girl on the street. In this world "the sell" is everything and still motivates what most websites do, and how they look. To a large extent this maybe true, but some characteristics of the web suggest that, as a medium, it may be moving, naturally and almost of its own accord, in a slightly different direction.

The parallels between the web and the art of memory show that the structured use of design is already mainstream on the web. The structure may currently be more vague than the art of memory recommends, but it is nevertheless a structure shaped by design. This is borne out in the kind of "wow factor" after which web designers strive and which user experience gurus champion. The most recent generation of websites covet this "wow factor" in a serious way. Sites that are "sexy" and "cool" have become not only aspirations for cutting-edge startups, but a requirement for more mainstream organisations. It might be argued that the logic of the user experience and the way this is shaping web design is already pushing it towards a form of communication (or "corporate" communication) which recognises the communication as an art form appreciated in its own right. Might, then, the logical outcome for the future be a website that is appreciated in the same way we appreciate Giotto or Caravaggio?

This situation shows up not only in the websites on public display, but in the people who create them. Working in web design studios, or even in corporate web teams, is often a little different from working in other corporate teams. Web teams tend to attract young idealistic people who are almost prepared to work flat out on a project in the belief they might change the face of modern culture. These are the sort of people that have traditionally been called "artists".

All of which begins to suggest that the world of the web contains fertile soil for an approach to communications which is both governed by a practical goal and artistic credentials. The industry has not reconciled these two characteristics entirely, and this might very well be some way off. But, speaking from the inside, it feels like a momentum is building in this direction.

It is scarcely defined and poorly understood intuitions like this that makes working with websites and online technologies so interesting. Anyone who knows even the slightest and slenderest technical detail can begin to sense that the web has potential with deep roots. The industry is certainly saturated with technologies, and marketers have invented every possible form of rhetorical bullshit you could imagine, but that's because they all have some sense of the seismic changes underfoot, and the opportunities these create.

The art of memory and "the art of memory"

If this is the case and the web also has something to learn from the art of memory, it's worth fanning the flames of artistic idealism a little. This brings us back to the art's origins in the macabre imagination of Simonides. It strikes me as no accident that all the ancient textbooks (as well as Frances Yates' history) begin with Simonides' tale of crushed corpses. It also strikes me as no accident that Simonides was a poet, that he conveyed the ideas of the art of memory as a story, and that this story is what we would think of today as a "horror" story.

The story of how Simonides discovered the art of memory is itself uniquely memorable. The images it creates stick in the mind, simply because they also stick in the gut. But the story also takes advantage of this power to create an order and unity which makes everything hang together. This combination of a powerful narrative with a purpose makes it more than just a horror story, and more than just a rhetorical trick; it makes it a piece of poetry that chimes like some cosmic cadence throughout the ages. It is an example of language and art aligned to human nature. It is, to cut it short, the perfect illustration of how art, in the grandest sense, can work in the way I have tried to describe.

Like for like with the state of advertising, marketing, corporate communications and other uses of art to convey a message or some kind of information, Simonides' story also emphasises a key difference. His story – his contribution to art – is powerful and memorable as a story. It's a story that someone might easily tell at a dinner party, or which, through greater elaboration, might become a short drama. The three-minute fillers between the "real" drama on TV that we sit through each day are, for the most part, not powerful or memorable pieces of art. Their overweening ambition is simply to sell, and, more often than not, much of their artistic merit is second-hand and derivative.

Not only are most corporate communications, by this reckoning, poor pieces of art, but, perhaps of greater concern to them, they are also comparatively poor pieces of communication. According to the art of memory's internal logic, the more striking and effective the image, the more memorable the object of recollection. This underlines the abject lack of imagination in most corporate communications. Which organisation, which business or government body would be prepared to associate its precious "brand" and public name with a dark and visceral story like the art of memory, or with any kind of story that doesn't wrap up its corporate name in the most ridiculous, banal and confectionery candy floss? The whole of the corporate world unthinkingly reflects a preening image of outrageously camp and comically overstated self-beautification! Most public bodies, if looked at objectively, wear grotesque masks smeared in inches of saffron mascara. Is everyone somehow enticed by this aesthetic when an organisation, rather than a person, adopts it? Why should we react differently to the appearances and persuasions of public life? Why should we not call it cheap and in poor taste?

The vicious circle of Aquinas' relational logic leads to a melancholy view of modern life. The company's or the government's view of something desirable is based on its own myopic vision, and its celebration of flimsy appearances makes its myopia look discerning. This world, this very insubstantial world, is the nested community in which most of us eat, sleep and breath. The way these organisations comport themselves in public sets the tone, and creates a public aesthetic and vocabulary, which, chosen or not, affects everyone. If a government or a business (even a charity) cannot tell a story except from its own point of view, how can anyone else except in private circumstances or from outside the status quo? This must mean that, for the most part, our collective health must be in decline?

But, by the same logic, this must also mean that there is an opportunity for any organisation with a bit more imagination. And it may be, given the curious state of the web and the conditions at this point in its evolution, that some brave organisation may just use the latest bit of kit to beat out a new path.

For some artists (established or aspiring) this imaginary future might seem liberating and exciting. For those that are already free from any corporate ties this might cause their hearts to sink. They might sense their conscripted return to the fold of a medieval guild. But this is not necessarily the natural conclusion to draw. In the model that Simonides leaves, the nature of the work of art must suit the goal at which it aims. This means that there are, at the very least, as many different works of art as there are goals. And the number of goals are only as limited as an imagination that can legitimately describe reality in desirable terms.

The question might then be: how far does that reality extend? Is it only as far as the practical ambitions of individuals, groups and organisations? Does nothing else have a goal or a purpose? Just as it is in the nature of a business to set its sights on a goal, surely many people have personal ambitions and objectives: to run a marathon, perhaps, or travel round the world? And in the same way it is surely also in their nature to pursue things like relationships, or defend their own intuition of right and wrong. Harder as it might be to discern – since a life as it is lived can never step back from itself – but a life or even simply "life" in an abstract sense, might be thought to have a desirable goal, or at least something comparable. Does this not mean that it too invites a suitable form of description to serve the goal? And, in the manner of Aquinas' bewildering specul-ation, why should it stop there?

Simonides invitingly daubs his story in this shade of metaphysical humility. He gave his eulogy to the gods, Castor and Pollux. But, in our society, everything about the way we think and communicate in public suggests we give ours to Scopas. And look how that turned out.

3.

Politics and the new rhetoric

A new rhetoric: essays on using the internet to communicate

How someone or something communicates matters. It matters because, either voluntarily or not, the communication will reveal something about the way they are thinking; and, more involuntarily than not, it will also reveal something about the culture and circumstances of what they are saying.

Close reading shows the mindset of authors, and, where political communication is concerned, institutions. So how something gets said is more than the decorative end to a process of firm or flimsy thought. Neither is it just an instrument for channelling a thought from one place to another. It reflects the instinct in the mind and body of the voice that's speaking.

If this is the case, then where communications concern the uses (or abuses) of power – or political rhetoric – close reading can never be far away from matters of social justice. What, then, does a "close reading" of political rhetoric in the new and always-changing digital sphere reveal?

Politics and the English language

Few have understood why communication matters better than George Orwell, and an overly conscientious reader of his famous essay, *Politics and the English Language*, might come away too intimidated to risk writing anything ever again. Orwell tries to demarcate clearly and precisely the relationship between politics and the use of language. He does not spell it out explicitly, but his argument hangs off a sturdy moral backbone and is, like much of his writing, fastidious about truth and truth-telling.

His concern is akin to the shape of his famous novel, *1984*. Just as Winston ultimately comes to love Big Brother, Orwell berates the indolence of modern culture for surrendering to the "lifeless imitative style" of received expressions and phraseology. At its most innocent, the targets of his attack are bad habits, and an idle frame of mind that can scarcely keep its head from crashing into the desk at the prospect it might be spurred onto the onerous activity of thought. To illuminate an object in the world, an idea or an opinion is difficult; it is easier to rely on stock phrases, tired metaphors and clichés. Modern English is assembled from pre-packaged parts which barely disguise the fact that the bulb inside the author's head is, at best, flickering. Instead it often "consists in gumming together long strips of words which have already been set in order by someone else".

This all becomes more insidious when language comes into contact with public affairs. If public language, or political language, is negligent in the way that Orwell describes, how can we hold it to account? If meaning in political language is elusive because its sequences of words are only "gummed together", in what sense can "public policy" form any kind of conversation with the "public"? The "lifeless imitative style" is the common characteristic of political literature, and a politician speaking in public – or a government writing through a public document such as a white paper – appears as a ventriloquist's dummy contrived to disguise the person and place at which the thought actually begins. In the same act of deception, it also robs all colour or character from the language. In one especially damning sentence, which neatly frames the dead eyes behind many political speeches, we read:

"The appropriate noises are coming out of his larynx, but his brain is not involved as it would be if he were choosing his words for himself."

Political language defaults to simply broadcasting the party line. And political rhetoric has no personality because it will not admit the company of individuals.

The "party line" can, of course, mean all sorts of different things. It might refer to the mantra of frontbench politicians who realise that the only way to communicate their views is through brain-boiling degrees of collective repetition. It might refer to the work of a government's faceless and phlegmatic bureaucracy. Or it might refer to something much worse: the abuse of political authority. Not too surprisingly, given the time at which he was writing, Orwell is most alert to the latter. Governments seize on the vagueness and imprecise use of words he has criticised when it is in their interest to defend the indefensible. At its most morally degenerate this becomes an abstract and overwrought style which blurs the edges of crimes committed by the state. He parodies:

"While freely conceding that the Soviet regime exhibits certain features which the humanitarian may be inclined to deplore, we must, I think, agree that a certain curtailment of the right to political opposition is an unavoidable concomitant of transitional periods, and that the rigors which the Russian people have been called upon to undergo have been amply justified in the sphere of concrete achievement."

Readers might think that the "concrete achievement" is too chillingly ironic to be anything more than a parody, but I am not so sure.

Clarity is Orwell's clear remedy. But it is clarity accompanied by a kind of vigilance. Winston's struggle against the all-seeing apparatus of Big Brother returns to view. To use language well is a fight. Some rhetorical habits are clearly bad: the passive voice, abstract constructions, metaphors the meaning of which have been forgotten, Marxist German translated into English, the Russian doll of clauses which Victorian English derived from its love of classical culture. But the essay's main injunction is "to let the meaning choose the word, and not the other way around". Which is another way of saying that writers should think before they write.

The note of moral urgency and sincerity in Orwell's essay leads him to devise a set of rules for any conscientious writer trying to crawl through the brambled hedgerows of modern English. These rules feel like he has assembled them in a very extemporary way, and the ink runs almost as soon as they have been committed to paper. The last rule reads "Break any of these rules sooner than say anything outright barbarous". The writer's own conscience also seems to upbraid himself, as he acknowledges that many of the vices of usage which he condemns he may have unwittingly adopted while writing the essay.

This underlying psychology is why taking Orwell at his word might make keeping schtum seem preferable to the muddle of forming a sentence. The difficulties of disentangling modern usage from lapsed imagery, archaisms, pretentious style, and the inst-ruction manual of packaged phrases give the impression that political rhetoric is something at which a writer will *inevitably* fail. As in *1984*, we, like Winston, will let our hearts beat for state surveillance.

What would Orwell make of "content strategy"?

But is this necessarily the case? Skipping over a mere forty years, Orwell's essay cues up the place of digital communications in public language nicely. With the advent of websites, governments in the 1990s were quick to start using them, whether for the delivery of public services or for public administration. They began by committing schoolboy errors: don't structure your information around the structure of your organisation, and produce content that suits the needs and character-istics of the people using the site. In England, this led to the creation of DirectGov and BusinessLink, and, in the last few years, the "single government domain" (www.gov.uk), managed and governed by an organ of the Cabinet Office, the Government Digital Service.

Orwell's essay is sometimes quoted by the (Orwellian-sounding) "thought leaders" of digital communications when they are enjoining the virtues of simplicity and clarity, but it would be, saying the least, naive to think that the quest for clarity online comes from a novelist whose views formed in the political turmoil and totalitarian despotisms of the early twentieth century. Most digital communications and marketing are practical. Businesses have something to sell, governments have policies to deliver, charities have causes to champion. Digital "channels" are an important tool in the rhetorical toolbox they deploy. The practicalities of using the new tool have, through research and experiment, underlined the need for simplicity and clarity, and shown the difference which clearly crafted content can make. So Orwell might not be a cause, but professionals who work with the government's digital content might recognise in him an ally to support the logic of their editorial task.

As is so often the case, private industry (working hand-in-hand and pocket-in-pocket with key areas of academia) pioneered much of the research that now informs a "user-centred" approach to web design. Among the many things that this research has considered it has looked closely, and repeatedly, at the way people read face-to-face with a computer screen. The pithy headline from the findings of this research has always been that they find it hard; and much harder than reading in print. (Among the many contributors to this research Jakob Nielsen and the work of the Nielsen Norman Group are among the best known.) People skim, scan, skip about, evincing something less than the staying power and intellectual commitment of a butterfly. The same is just as true of the way they respond to multimedia. Two and a half hour lectures are out. Videos should last no longer than two minutes. The search for gratification is impossibly impatient, restless and hedonistic.

All of this means that the whole trajectory of digital communications is towards the kind of clarity, concision, and focus about which Orwell was so in earnest. The lobotomised attention-span means that text online is stripped down to fit within the compressed space that readers are willing to accept. All long words are abolished. All long sentences are only allowed in downloadable documents which people can print out. Pages should break up points in any sequence into bulleted lists. Paragraphs should be no more than two sentences; and the page – just in case your eyes might be about to start abusing the compliance procedures of your brain – needs breaking down into clearly marked headings. "Writing for the web" is, in short, an easily transferable skill for anyone who might want to teach eight year olds.

Given the Scotch broth into which many organisations unavoidably slop whenever they try to say anything, the discipline which writing for the web requires might be something to encourage. Certainly by Orwell's standards, the work of the Government Digital Service has untangled the convoluted skein of bureaucratic procedure into a model of lucidity. Gov.uk brings together public services and information in a single place, written in prose pared down to forestall the question in the mind of the reader – or "user" – before they have even thought it. This all comes from careful analysis of the archetypal psychology that Government meets when it offers services and information.

So far as the practice of government is concerned, the migraine that trawling through lines of backlit text induces appears to have more or less forced the government in England to adopt something secondarily related to George Orwell's prescription for political language. Worked out through an ethic of consumer (if not public) service, it tries its hardest to make Leviathan directly accountable to the needs of citizens "transacting" with the state.

So much, then, for practice, but what about persuasion? Helping people to understand their consumer rights is one thing; grabbing their attention and influencing their behaviour is another. The purpose of the communication might be different, but the character of the content is cognate. An impatient, restless and hedonistic glance at the websites for the main political parties in England shows straight away how far the same model of communication obtains, albeit governed by a different strategy. It seems clear that this "glance" should deliver a succinct summary of the party's position on key areas of public policy, with a bulleted list of actions which shows how they will put their position to task. And if you can't be bothered to read line by line, keywords or phrases are usually in bold.

It is a commonplace of user research that imagery and video "drive engagement", so it is not too surprising to find videos of party leaders, either summarising their stance or anxiously demonstrating their energetic activity in some ideologically critical part of the *res publica*. But a stricture of the same research is that "users" rarely watch for more than two minutes, which means that any footage is brutally clipped. Video content is the search for a catchy sound bite which illuminates one patch of grass for the dimly lit face of a herd animal before they move on.

These websites also satisfy Orwell's disdain for platitudes and abstractions. Most political parties are at pains to show that the work of the party is far from a pamphlet of empty pledges, but has a direct bearing on the lives of individuals and communities. Taking advantage of geo-search technology, they now allow users to punch in their postcode and see, in practical terms, what the party is doing for them, and who at a local level is responsible.

Indeed, in theory at least, the widespread adoption of social media also means that most forms of politicking through digital channels are personal. Politicians groom their Twitter and Facebook accounts in the same way they pick their wardrobe. I find it hard to imagine that most people are anything less than cynical about the sincerity of their presence on these channels, but, to the extent that they say anything substantial through them, it becomes easy to clearly trace back a statement to the decisions of an individual. The word "engagement" may quickly suffocate in the atmosphere of political spin, but it at least gives political rhetoric the *appearance* of something which originates with people rather than a press officer's backroom boilerplate.

But perhaps to frame the "social media revolution" in this way is misleading, and assumes a "them and us" divide which social media, of its own initiative, has managed to cross. It has, in other words, created a deeper shift in political dialogue. The sheer scale and clamour of social media mean that a presence on the key channels for governments, their politicians and political parties is not just an opportunity they need to seize strategically, but more or less a tacit requirement of democratic accountability. Or, in a more hard-nosed fashion, governments are hard-pushed to ignore anything significant that happens on social media.

As Eric Schmidt and Jared Cohen have pointed out in *The New Digital Age*, citizens frequently seize on matters of public concern before the lubberly beast of government can stir itself to life. This means that the contemporary current should carry through the mood of cynicism to a more satisfactory outcome; governments and their politicians, so long as they permit the freedom that social media assumes, must find ways to talk and behave in online communities which do *not* elicit cynicism. To stand aloof is not an option.

Digital technology seems, once again, to have answered even the deepest and most apocalyptic of Orwell's worries about political language. Governments simply cannot control and manage a "message" or an interpretation of events centrally. If the line they take is at odds with the events as they affect citizens, they will get found out. So social media means that propaganda has a much harder time of it. For parts of the world where the political settlement is closer to the dynamic of Orwell's Europe in the 1940s – where authoritarianism and the vested interests of the state exert pressure on the body politic – social media is a genuine asset (even where the government places restrictions on its use).

Schmidt and Cohen cite the example of China. When the Chinese government tried to manage reporting after a rail crash in 2011, and restrict investigation into its causes, members of the Chinese *weibo* network were quick to point out the government's machinations and expose that the cause was due to a design flaw and expedited public infrastructure projects.

The picture that is beginning to emerge looks very optimistic (if a little one-sided). If digital communications are judged against Orwell's standard for political rhetoric, we might even risk a cry of celebration. They have pushed public administration and political accountability towards greater transparency. Some online public communications might still default to the thickly whipped language of bureaucratic or political protocol. But this looks uncomfortable shoulder-to-shoulder with the nature of digital communications, which, if they are to work at all, seem to demand a level of clarity and focus. Even where the present is gloomy, if the future is digital, the outlook might look brighter.

The "arduous business"

So is it all good news? Many of Orwell's rules digital copywriters would, as we have seen, embrace: short sentences, a preference for Anglo-Saxon over Latinate words and phrases, the active not passive voice, and a duty of care towards the needs of readers. All of which help us dodge the quagmire of brain death which comes when language chooses the author and not the other way around. I have already suggested that there is something morally impatient about Orwell. He was, beyond his writing, someone wrestling with the harsh realities that give rise to questions of social and political justice. This means that all his writing begins from a powerfully held sense of truth and the moral equilibrium on which its illuminations depend. Read by the light of Orwell's character, this is, at the very least, implicit in the essay. So, given that digital communications seem to be quite good at following the essay's rules, does this mean that they satisfy the moral concern that the rules protect?

I would suggest that asking this question exposes an unresolved tension that is unresolved because Orwell's clarion call is as much impatient as it is moral, and because the tension will not admit the kind of unsullied or "unmediated" resolution for which Orwell is impatiently casting about. Read intellectually Orwell is a nominalist. Read sensibly – in context – he is a realist. All of which means that the answer to the last question is not straight-forward to answer without a clearer moral framework to govern the purpose and probity of political rhetoric. The substance and character of the essay does not offer this kind of broader vision in any detail.

The plainly held exhortation "to let the meaning choose the word, and not the other way around" suggests a way of thinking which reaches back to a richer and well-developed heritage of thought about the nature, purpose and place of rhetoric: the ancient world.

Aristotle, with the slightly fusty tone of a seasoned scholar, opens *The Art of Rhetoric* with a definition that is roughly analogous to Orwell's position:

"Let rhetoric be the power to observe the persuasiveness of which any particular matter admits."

This definition, which serves throughout the discussion that ensues, post-dates a more lively discussion about the nature of rhetoric thematised in a number of Plato's dialogues, but especially *Phaedrus* and *Gorgias*. Here we witness a dialectical dance over the nature, even the soul, of rhetoric. Its cryptic conclusion allows Aristotle to build from his first premise, but leaves the reader with the impression that Plato felt the same need for vigilance as Orwell. Something moral, chime Plato and Orwell across the ages, is at stake in the use of language.

Stopping some way short of close academic scrutiny, it is still possible to see in the Platonic dialogues a broad outlook that expands the search from which Orwell's essay begins. Certainly Plato provides a more developed account of rhetoric, but one that is, if anything, even more "vigilant". Or, perhaps, it is more than vigilant. At one point in *Gorgias*, Socrates calls rhetoric "contemptible", which shows that he has high standards for political language (even, and by his own admission, impossibly high standards). For the plot of *Gorgias*, these standards come into conflict with the art of oratory and sophistry conceived as something like a profession among the legal and political customs of the day. Socrates arrives fashionably (or disdainfully?) late to a dinner party where the famous orator *Gorgias* has just finished speaking. He then spends the dialogue overturning the money tables, by going head to head with three champions of a morally unscrupulous and sophistical view of oratory and the art of persuasion.

In both *Gorgias* and *Phaedrus,* Plato combats basically the same understanding of rhetoric as "an agent of the kind of persuasion which is designed to produce conviction, but not to educate people, about matters of right and wrong." Throughout Socrates belittles the trophies that skilful rhetoric claims: that it confers the most knowledge, power, pleasure and happiness. The self-interested and morally promiscuous view that to persuade with no regard for virtue is muddle-headed and compromises morality and true happiness with short-term thinking that is, ultimately, divided against itself. Rhetoric, in so far as it concerns public matters and morality, cannot pursue an "immoral" case without conceding an a priori knowledge of virtue; and this conflicts with the claim that a rhetorician is free to persuade non-experts of anything. A rhetorician can no more do this than a doctor can practise medicine with no knowledge of human physiology. Rhetoric practised in this way is a skilful "knack" that is designed to flatter, but its returns are illusory. A politician or a dictator who wins over the citizenry by means of flattery is, effectively, in hock to their subjects rather than free to pursue their own fate.

Running throughout *Gorgias* is a sense that the pursuit of rhetoric as a narrow "agent of persuasion" starts from a narrow view of life; but that true virtue, and so true happiness, depend on a broader account of how things stand. The end of *Gorgias* makes it clear that a grounding in virtue must precede the application of rhetoric; but the mood of Socrates' language – perhaps responding to the dogged instrumentalism of his opponents and the culture for which they speak – is sceptical. He bemoans that "we strut around as if we were important, when we are so far from understanding things that we never think the same thought twice about the same issues". If Plato admits any place for rhetoric in his philosophy, the tenor at this point is stronger than just vigilance, but something more like extreme caution.

Phaedrus picks up the theme of rhetoric, but in the context of a discussion about, and suffused with, the true meaning of love. Socrates encounters Phaedrus – a young student of rhetoric – outside the walls of Athens, cogitating on a speech written about the practicalities and utility of seduction. The circumstance prompts an extended discussion about the nature of love (via the content of the first speech written by the off-stage Lysias, and two speeches improvised by Socrates). The dialogue then rolls over to rhetoric and stigmatises it in the same way as an "unsystematic knack" of persuasion not informed by any real knowledge. It holds out more hope, all the same, that it is "not shameful in itself" provided it is done well. So what does it mean to do it well?

The parallel themes (of love and rhetoric) in *Phaedrus*, have sometimes given the impression that the dialogue is not thematically unified. But the same "love of wisdom" coordinates the "dialectical" character and trajectory of the two segments. The first part of the discussion moves from a view of love as an essentially erotic and mutually convenient business arrangement, to a view of love as "love of wisdom" (or "philosophy"), in which two lovers guide each other – as Socrates and Phaedrus do in the dialogue – in self-disciplined study to "recollect" the true nature of reality contained and consecrated through the immortal part of human nature: the soul. In the second part of the discussion, Socrates answers the question asked of rhetoric in the same way as in *Gorgias* but with reference to the fuller and more imaginative vision of reality with which the first half of the dialogue concludes.

Challenging rhetoric as sophistry, Socrates argues that to speak and write well, the speaker or author must distinguish between a superficial and true account of things, even drawing the same analogy with medicine as a skill that depends on knowledge of the body. The difference with *Gorgias* is that the first half of *Phaedrus* supplies a much richer account of the "body" knowledge of which will admit persuasion. This allows Socrates to state much more openly that good rhetoric depends on an embodied view which refracts metaphysical reality, with all its complexities and idiosyncrasies.

Human beings are, for Socrates, constituted as body and soul. This – metaphysical – anatomy can draw human beings in different directions, either, chaotically, under the meandering, self-interested and lustful designs of the body, or by listening to the memory of "the things which our souls once saw during their journey as companions to a god".

"Soul" is a problematic word in modern usage and fraught with connotations, but, for Plato, it has a dual meaning. It is both the part of human nature that recalls the immortal good (the part that grounds human life in a superabundant metaphysical reality), but also the animating breath of life that distinguishes and defines the character of a human being. *This* is the reality – the reality of the "many" grounded in the "one" – with which rhetoric must come to terms, and, as Phaedrus somewhat wearily observes, as a form of expertise it "does seem to be quite an arduous business".

Phaedrus isn't kidding. Socrates sets out just how challenging the rhetorician's task really is. A true rhetorician must grasp and be attentive to the idiosyncratic character of people and the world they inhabit before they can put their words to any sensible or moral use. We read at length:

"Once our would-be orator has a good intellectual understanding of all this, he should next observe souls actually involved in and being affected by events, using his senses to pay keen attention to them, or else he won't yet be gaining anything from the discussions he heard at school. When he cannot only say what kind of person is persuaded by what kind of speech, but also spot that kind of person before him and tell himself that here, in real life and before his eyes, is the kind of person and the kind of character which was the subject of those earlier discussions, and to which such-and-such a kind of speech should be applied in such-and-such a way to persuade him of such-and-such – once he is capable of doing all this, and moreover has understood the proper moments for speaking and for keeping quiet, and can also recognize the appropriate and inappropriate occasions for concision, arousing pity, shocking the audience, and all the various modes of speech he has learnt, then and only then will his expertise have been perfected and completed."

It is a trite point but the Platonic dialogues are two and a half thousand years old. For those with a relativist bent of mind, this might well put them beyond the reach of any contemporary use, much less use in the context of something as new and newfangled as digital communications. Modern usage is also loaded with so many secular assumptions that terms like "soul" and "metaphysical reality" look automatically and inescapably arcane and anachronistic. By way of an attempt at cultural translation – with all the familiar casualties that entail – Plato, in a very simple sense, is really just saying that rhetoric, or for our purposes political communication, must begin from a sensitive understanding of reality. Or, to put it another way, rhetoric is most persuasive where it begins with the truth. The "arcana" arise in the picture of reality and the obscurely crafted, but beautifully realised, imagery he paints.

To give more dimension and texture to the line and figure of this notion, albeit with liberal brush-strokes, the place of political rhetoric might be likened to the job of an artistic director in the theatre. The play – the work of a "creative genius" – represents the beautiful reality our rhetoric must first understand if we are to do things well. In the theatre it is sometimes said that there are broadly two ways to direct a play (notwithstanding nuances and, no doubt, many differences of technique). Either the director can respect the integrity and quality of the play and see it as their task to coax it into expression on the stage, or they can use it as the raw materials for their own interpretation, message or creative insight ("*Timon of Athens* as a statement about western materialism in the late twentieth century"). Plato's prescription for rhetoric is akin to the former rather than the latter; it begins out of profound respect and admiration for the world (understood in the correct way) that it must channel and celebrate. The agitprop sophistry of the latter wants to own, demarcate and enfold reality within a spurious vision that is intrinsically wanting in moral and intellectual imagination, to the extent that it shrouds and alienates all concerned from things that are valuable and good.

Whatever a reader might think of Plato's "love of wisdom" – and it has, unsurprisingly, produced diametrically opposed interpretations – it is a poetic and imaginatively rich piece of metaphysical speculation. It is, as a piece of rhetoric, remarkable. *Phaedrus* especially is a text with many subtle layerings and rhetorical flourishes that strike a peculiarly resonant note. It is a work of literature that appeals to human curiosity and invites repeated and renewed examination. This, in itself, shows that it is the very thing it enjoins rhetoric to be: born of curiosity.

A simple question will help to steer the discussion back to the wider topic: would anyone say the same thing about digital communications for political purposes? (Or even digital communications as such?) My fairly confident assertion is that the answer to this question is largely "no". They might be all the things that Orwell, in his pan-fried list, wants them to be – clear, concise, polite, targeted – but they are, overwhelmingly and in one variety or another, functional rather than curious about the nature of the world around them. And, sadly, by the dimly distant light of Plato's illuminating soul, they are often spectacularly uninteresting and morally and spiritually dead.

Most political rhetoric online is deliberately about as textured and idiosyncratic as a Babybel, precisely because it needs to meet the rules that digital copywriting, following the nature of the technology, demands. Web pages are typically pared down to assume that readers will scan through them until their attention is caught by something else. Blog posts are similarly designed to distil a matter into little more than a few hundred words; their diminutive cousins on social media channels might share a rousing infographic or a short snippet of video curated for interest, but the scrutiny of the content is similarly ephemeral. If characters, places, and the ambiguous knot of circumstance occur, they do so like advertisements we momentarily glimpse from the moving window of a car.

Part of this must be explained by the laziness that the technology provokes; that people find it harder to read online and are more likely to scan. The finely sliced feast of content also means that they don't have to spend too much time chewing over the same thing. But is there something more culturally discreet and spectral at work?

Modern minds typically have a conceited outlook; they want to consume everything, to see everything, to climb to the vantage point which commands a panoramic view. They are elevated in a fiercely observing posture above everything else. The internet is a delectable prospect for this appetite, since it provides access to *more* in every possible sense: more data and knowledge, consumption, pleasure, people, power and so on. But surely the puritanically pithy nature of digital content bears only the peculiar imprint of lives which are much the same shape as they have always been. We can only do so much. Married to vaunting ambition and inflated opportunity, the more we do, the less we do things justice. The internet is *La Grande Bouffe* and openly invites us to gorge ourselves to death.

This is radically at odds with the psychology of a mind married to differentiation and context – or a *prudent* mind in the classical sense of the word – which Socrates recommends to his intellectual "lover". Socrates' psychology, for all its apparent "arcana", turns out to be the more realistic, and, in the fashion of Attic prudence, practical. The kind of "pragmatism" which is either the standard boast or instruction of most "thought leaders" shaping digital content actually dissimulates a grossly, even grotesquely, unrealistic and distorted view of what we are capable (or, at a deeper level, simply what we are). Either it assumes that we are capable of assimilating the universe of data on the internet and necessarily reduces it to the fleeting shadow across the surface of an eye, or it admits our limitations and works to nominal constraints that are no less transitory (and, by their nature, no more meaningful). Both fail to grasp what Socrates urges Phaedrus to grasp – "souls involved in being affected by events".

Notice the difference with Orwell's rules and the rules of writing for the web; Plato does not say "always be concise". First the author must judge the context (or the "soul"), and then find the appropriate way to communicate (which, depending on the circumstance, *could* demand that the orator is concise). The rules of rhetoric are as flexible as the manifold forms that reality can take. When we glimpse this way of thinking through the prevailing culture of digital content, it looks hard. And it is hard. It requires thought, care, attention, subtlety, an appreciation for the richness of characters and circumstances which lend life its colour and contrast. Digital content, in juxtaposition, is relatively easy; it is more or less a pattern which can be iterated at the click of a button. It is a simple set of rules which have the same, simple character, regenerated programmatically to produce a featureless desert. For Plato, communicating should be an act of consecration; for digital content, in its current state, it is an instruction manual in nihilism or how to purge things of their given meaning and value.

This might all sound rarefied, so let's make it plain by picking up some of the examples I have already mentioned. Take the digital presence of the main political parties in the UK. I would suggest that by looking at the websites for the Conservative, Labour or Liberal Democrat parties, we would not be able to distinguish the character of one from the other. The character, values, personality and governing philosophy of each party are not so much identical as invisible. If a reader were to make an attempt at differentiating, they would be forced to study the party's pledge on VAT or an adjustment to tuition fees. They might even fall back on the banalities of the latest exorbitantly commissioned but vacuous party slogan.

The role of each website is, in other words, functional: it exists to provide access to the messages of the party (just as ecommerce sites exist to facilitate a transaction). The design, style of writing, use of imagery and multimedia – the *rhetoric* – is entirely instrumental, which is why all the sites are more or less identical, and more or less identical to any other site with a professional purpose. In Plato's terms this is pure sophistry. This way of doing business – business and politics are on this point, logically speaking, identical – assumes that a reader or user of the site will differentiate between the Conservatives and Labour by their "product" or what they say. By commodifying meaning they set it apart (almost as though it could be dressed in designer wrapping and transported freely from one place to another).

In Plato's description, and arguably in the spirit – but not the letter – of Orwell's writing, meaning cannot be abstracted from a context. This can no more be done than a doctor can practise medicine apart from knowledge of the human body. And to sport meaning in this kind of masquerade must be a disruptive, manipulative and violent act, which, ultimately sterilises or cauterises the political debate. The effect is not a dialogue, or a living piece of dialectic, but mechanised voices which "talk" to no-one. A more accurate, but brutal, image to characterise this sort of meaning might be to describe it as a severed head which we carry around in a Louis Vuitton handbag. The kind of "democratic discussion" this form of necrophiliac rhetoric assumes is akin to the black comedy of two dismembered heads trying to hold a conversation.

If this seems overstated and histrionic, think about this cultural trope in wider forms of political rhetoric. I am not suggesting that there is something special about internet technologies which divest language of meaning, but that our use of the internet reflects back at us cultural assumptions which do. The same assumptions permeate most forms of public rhetoric. Take the television "debates" for the UK general election. Watching each party leader talk, the viewer couldn't help but feel sorry for them as they struggled to realise whether they were talking to the television audience, the host or the camera (sometimes in the course of a single sentence). It was a lot like watching a small group of individuals stand in a room full of people and talk at no-one in particular. This is the sort of behaviour that we would ordinarily say might warrant special treatment. Were these really debates or, in fact, a socially acceptable form of insanity?

Political rhetoric "talks to no-one" (and consequently often turns into a cacophony of voices talking over each other) because it is usually removed from a context, in much the way it is on most websites. The problem with political rhetoric, which is reflected in concentrated and extreme form online, is that it is dead.

If persuading someone means transmitting a determinate and fixed package of content from one place to another, it is easy to see how the same business arrangement obtains in the relationship citizens have with the state. The state provides services for the benefit of either the general public or specific parts of it. A service, by its nature, has an instrumental character, with the service provider at one end and the "customer" or "client" at the other. Increasingly digital technology is a common way in which a transaction between these two parties takes place.

Most civilised societies would recognise that the state, in some form, needs to deliver some public services, and if internet technologies can play their part, then sites like gov.uk are more or less a lesson in best practice. The character of communication, here, is similarly "practical", fixed not on the people involved but an object – a tax return, a student loan, a welfare payment – administered between two parties. Its mechanical nature, however efficient and user friendly, is also similarly impersonal.

It is curious that in the short history of Government online, we have, following the logic of the user experience, found our way to the notion of the single government domain. Life began with a website for each government department and each government agency, with a team and a budget to manage and administer their activity. When the government explored how this structure of information worked for citizens interacting with government they were, unsurprisingly, confused. Ordinary people, in their innocence, did not know that one process was the responsibility of the Home Office and another process the responsibility of the National Crime Agency Remuneration Review Body (duh!). They just saw "Government" with a capital "G".

By putting the needs of citizens first, the proposal for a single domain revealed the real character of the relationship that many members of the public have with their government. This is a relationship described and elaborated by many "state of nature" political theorists. The state of human nature necessitates a "contract" of some sort with a powerful, and if necessary overbearing, executive authority to preserve the order and interests of society. Government is a big thing "out there" that we vote for and which (if we are lucky) does things for us.

The relationship that a citizen has with government in this kind of arrangement is similar to the relationship they might have with their insurance company. You are unlikely to hold a sustained, engaging, or even interesting, conversation with a salesperson reading from a script in a call centre, but they will do things for you, under the direction of their anonymous supervisors, based on your ability to pay, and the legal framework that governs this sort of transaction. Substitute the word "pay" for "vote" and we get something like a contractual theory of government.

The single government domain sits on a cultural and political *assumption* that you will put to one side all the many rounded, various, odd, beguiling and circumstantial things that define and characterise you as a person – all the things that Plato succinctly sums up in his mysterious little word "soul" – when you are having a conversation with "Government". But providing government services online does at least involve more than one voice; it's just that the voices are conversing in the cold and self-centred atmosphere of a transaction. There is something clipped, maybe even frosty, about the character of the single government domain.

What's more meaningful than talking to a jelly fish?

Public services are, of course, much more significant than the picture we can glimpse through gov.uk. The big domestic issues are healthcare, education, welfare, transport and so on. And the relationship between citizen and state in these areas does, typically, turn on more meaningful exchanges: the relationship a pupil has to their teacher, a patient to their doctor, or someone in a parlous state to their social worker. Since it is in these relationships that public money should translate into an impact on people's lives, then surely the priority for digital communications and technology should be the ways in which it can support them and, like the artistic director massaging Euripides' text to life, coax them into their fullest expression?

This, then, begs a question: are government and its associated agencies best placed to make this sort of judgement? Does Ofsted, or an equivalent body, know best how a teacher should work with a pupil? If people are as idiosyncratic as Plato suggests, then surely this depends on contextual judgement and the self-governing arrangements at the school or in a dialogue across a broader civil association of practice. Would it not make most sense to empower those in the cut and thrust of these relationships to self-determine the most effective way to do their work (including how they might use new technologies like the web)? To refer this judgement up a political hierarchy only subordinates the particular circumstance of pupil and teacher to the more indiscriminate perspective of an official at a government agency. Unless government agencies have some sort of unmediated access to truth that elude lesser mortals, it's hard not to see this sort of subservience as, intentionally or unintentionally, political and aggressive.

Empowering "frontline" public services is not a new idea. And a corollary of it must be that public servants have the autonomy to manage how they communicate. It follows that as schools, the NHS, and social services become more directly accountable to their local communities, they start to explore the best ways to manage these relationships. The logic of this position means they should be free to do so. So there is no prior rule to determine the shape and character of public servants communicating with the public, since it should take many and varied forms. Websites, social media, among other communications channels, simply need to adapt to the circumstance.

This is more or less an unremarkable conclusion, since to some extent at least, it has always happened. Still, it begins to reflect back on the relationship that citizens can have, if any, with central government, the political elite and the debate about public policy. If people and parliament can only hold a meaningful conversation over the fence of frontline services, then it tells us a little about what the word "meaningful" means for public debate.

It tells us that legislation, fiscal policy, the graceful swoop of a socially minded nostrum, the gobbling noises which accompany the scrutiny of bills, debates, interviews, manifestos, white papers, committee hearings, National Audit Office reports, only "come to life" in the bearing they have on the orbit of activity in which I live, breathe and function, because this is the only lexicon of meaning available to me. Unless someone can translate the annualised Resource Accounting and Budgeting charge into an experience in which I have a stake, then it will remain exactly what it sounds like: a piece of technocratic jargon which might exercise policy wonks but provides most sane people with an excuse to lean peacefully into a yawn. It tells us that political debate is only meaningful in the way that Socrates discussed with Phaedrus.

In a liberal democracy, politicians cannot be so complacent about technocratic jargon. They have to seduce the electorate, which means learning to speak plainly about such matters. It also sires an entire professional class: political journalists. In romantic lore political journalists are meant to flirt in an internecine affair with the Machiavellian princes who strut the corridors of power. Out of this masochistic marriage we – the public – witness their progeny: public transparency.

But is the sort of hard-won rhetoric which passes for public transparency meaningful for me and my parochial little life? It is a working assumption of liberal democracy that it is; and, in a double-wrapping of assumption, it also implies the same psychology of meaning abstracted from context. Human beings have brains which use words and the meaning of those words can escape the particulars of the place they are first uttered. The political candidate needs only a hotline to the press, or the right kind of microphone, to voice a policy and I will be able to understand them and make an "informed" choice about whether they are suitable to govern.

To summarise, human beings are really decision -making machines, and communication just hooks up one locus of decision-making to another. It is no accident that political websites have this character. They just reflect the prevailing culture which fetishizes the "message" above everything else. Life as a citizen in a liberal democracy is fairly easy. All you need to do is sit there and watch, read or listen. Life as a politician creates monsters of adrenalin, who try to be all things to all people simultaneously. In the same way we want to do everything through the internet we also, farcically and rather perversely, want David Cameron to be ubiquitous. Which mercifully, for him and us, is not possible. Is it any wonder they say that all political careers end in failure?

So what we call "public transparency" is not really all that meaningful to me in my parochial little life. If meaning is mediated through my horizons, most cheerfully we might say that a conversation with a senior politician is more meaningful than one I might have with a jelly fish.

In the frame of such a colourful picture, a bright future for political rhetoric, wished through the changes of digital technology, begins to a look a little premature. So is there any glimmer of hope?

A knotted thread in the preceding argument is that digital communications often just adapt to the conventions and customs of public dialogue. Perhaps this means they need re-imagining. Or perhaps, they are already straining at the boundaries of established practice and we just need to set them free?

So many different strands and traits of the internet show its potential to illuminate political reality in forceful and searching ways. Yet, time after time, it just reinvents itself in prettier and prettier forms of bland business-speak which think of automaton-like "users" only as utility-maximising agents.

The internet, in its current shape, is similar to George Orwell and the problems of his famous essay. The reason Orwell is such an interesting writer through which to examine the question of political rhetoric is, as I have already indicated, because all his thoughts are not so much pricked as mortally wounded by conscience. And yet, in his remedy for political rhetoric, he resorts to a formula or a set of nominal rules to govern the use and meaning of language. He thereby betrays the same "formulaic" habit of mind we can see rabidly at work in the virtual world.

Orwell's concern for social injustice, inequalities, poverty, power, politics, imperialism, political hypocrisy mean that his writing is, as a whole, rich and rounded; it opens out to expose a full and frank portrayal of particular people in particular places living with the consequences of social and political reality. These penned insights are not reducible to the set of nominal rules at which he clutches in his despair over the decadence of public words.

Like Orwell, the spirit, but not the letter, of the internet wants to enrich the picture up to the horizon. It does this in two principal ways: by giving us a deeper understanding of it, and the means to engage with it.

There are now many examples to show how local communities have used social networks to marshal and galvanise a community, sometimes, as in the case of the 2012 UK riots, not for a constructive purpose.

But to place a positive spin on even that example, at the time of the UK riots, I was living streets away from the Stokes Croft area of Bristol where the Bristol riots took place. I had turned in for the night at about midnight and shortly after was woken by the sound of a police helicopter shaking the walls of my building. Peering tentatively out the window, I saw mounted police charging down my street, chasing, what turned out to be, fourteen year-olds pretending to be ninjas. Stokes Croft is a self-consciously unconventional and anti-establishment place, but this was, I thought, a step up from an anarchist book fair run by the *People's Front of Stokes Croft*. Something was afoot. So I checked the BBC Bristol website. Nothing there. I checked the *Bristol Evening Post*. Nothing there. Then I started searching on Twitter, and from the combined comments of local residents, I could piece together what was going on.

So what does this tell us? For one thing it shows how easily social media can undercut traditional forms of reporting. A local area was affected by a significant event. People, almost immediately, took to their phones, posting details, photos, short videos of the events as they happened. The traditional forms of media only managed to provide this description of the facts much later.

But, as we know, reporting in the media does more than simply provide the facts. It also invites opinion as the facts crystallise. Opinion often tries to enlist the help of an "expert", but the history of opinion pieces testify to opinions across the wide spectrum of "expertise". Media organisations have editorial values - or, in some cases, institutionalised bias - and these values will often colour the kind of opinions which vie for attention. Social media is, to say the very least, also opinionated; but on a platform like Twitter you will hear the full range of opinions: ill-informed, strident, big-oted, intelligent, outrageous (and outraged), surreal, ironic, expert … the list could continue without stopping short of most adjectives in our, or any, language.

To draw a comparison, then, the reports I later read (or watched) from the traditional media organisations did not expand the picture of events available on social media. One tweet might have contradicted another or misreported something, but, read collectively, they provided an accurate account of what was going on. And the traditional news items also provided a much more slanted perspective than the more democratic range of interpretation flushed out in the form of the sublime and the ridiculous on Twitter. So, in this example, Twitter had provided me with at least as much information, in a fairer and more representative fashion, and much quicker than the rear-drear and eye-tinted professional journalists.

This sort of example is hardly new. It is even a little too familiar. Commentators have been documenting the power of user-generated content since at least President Obama's first election campaign. People in most communities with any kind of access to social media will be able to cite their own examples of how it has helped to organise, galvanise and inform people in the community. And this will encompass the full range of social and antisocial behaviour, as well as serious and trivial matters.

Neither should we think just in terms of social media and its best-known platforms. It bears repeating that the internet was originally a way in which scientists could share their notes. Just as those empirically rigorous notes helped the scientific community to form a better collective understanding of the problems under examination, it stands to reason that the internet, and digital technology generally, should allow members of the public to scrutinise the public polis in a similar way. Government at national and local level is committed to publishing information for the benefit of citizens, increasingly under the same "transactional" mantra of gov.uk. Local charities, professional and civil societies, and community organisations will typically all have some kind of online presence, which should help to collate and share information about activities, issues, or simply the nature of different areas.

This comes back, via a long route, to a Queen cliché: the amount of information about the public realm has grown extraordinarily. With specific commitments to publishing more data in open and structured formats, public assets of information have also become more easily accessible and open to sophisticated analysis. The data.gov.uk website indexes datasets published right across the public sector in the UK at national and local level, and, though it has fought a battle to do so, publishes them according to open and machine-readable standards.

Social media, which is now a vital organ for digital communications, means that the work of Councils, consultations on policy, information about the local environment (and so on …), invite members of the public to become involved, take the information, and even transform it in new ways to expand and improve public discourse.

Towards the end of *Phaedrus*, just as the dialogue sinks wearily into the tasks of rhetoric, the discussion draws into the open one of its lurking themes: the difference between speech and writing, or the *form* that rhetoric takes. Since we are reading a "dialogue" it comes as no surprise to find that Socrates extols speech above writing. If trying to make language meaningful outside its immediate context is fundamentally destructive, Socrates seems to say that the act of writing is the weapon which finally puts it in the ground. He introduces the subject through an Egyptian myth, according to which writing was discovered as a "science" to improve memory and intelligence. The myth quickly turns against this claim:

"It will atrophy people's memories. Trust in writing will make them remember things by relying on marks made by others, from outside themselves, not on their own inner resources, and so writing will make the things they have learnt disappear from their minds."

The vain attempt to capture and preserve meaning in written marks has the opposite effect; it turns it into the epitaph on a tombstone. The written form bears the vestige of thoughts that were once alive, but if we ask it to talk back to us, it will remain "aloof in silence". By trying to objectify meaning, writing destroys it, because it loses the person and place – the context – in which it was first uttered.

If we accept this characterisation, then surely the nature of digital communications is uniquely well placed to make public dialogue much more meaningful than it has ever been. First, it reveals more about the world, mediated through the circumstances of particular individuals and communities. Second, it does so horiz-ontally, as a dialogue across and between those communities, rather than vertically with an artificially elevated political class. Social media, if pushed, provides a framework in which language can come to life, rather than quietly fade in sclerotic and sterile propaganda.

If, however, the conditions of the digital landscape are fertile terrain for a more meaningful reckoning with the public sphere, some people might demur at the suggestion that it has borne much fruit.

Does anyone rely solely on the information citizens provide on twitter as the authoritative source of current affairs? How reliable and trustworthy is the information about public life that is available online? How easy to locate and understand is the same information? How well-presented and engaging is it? And, in practice, how many people would actually hunt out content published by public sector organisations, or scrutinise their data? How comfortable would many people feel about voicing their views on social media, given the vociferous, sometimes criminally violent, "no holds barred" nature of public behaviour online?

Anarchist subversion of the streets of Stokes Croft shows that social media really comes to life over issues that touch people's lives. If something flares up for a local community it will be all over the networks in a matter of minutes. But for most people Twitter, Facebook and their rivals have not undermined trad-itional forms of media and reporting on current affairs. Even seasoned students of public policy, are unlikely to rely on the information they can get from the Office for

National Statistics, the Department for Work and Pensions or the data.gov.uk website, if someone has already synthesised this for them.

In a sense the question might be: even though digital tools allow me to interrogate the world immediately around me, why should I? What's the point? What difference will it make? The institutions of government – the departments of state, the national agencies, and, of course, parliament – are far removed, remote bodies run by a tiny, and often privileged, elite. The community that social media empowers ultimately has little realistic purchase over the bureaucratic machinery and "sophisticated" development and implementation of policy for which it is responsible. So is this chalk and cheese? Digital technologies want us to take more direct ownership of the public estate, but the nature and character of public institutions resist. Contractual government and digital communications are, in spirit, at odds with each other.

So we are suspended between two states – the old world and the new. Digital communications as a new form of rhetoric is a radical challenge not just to the traditional forms of media management and "messaging", but, at a deeper level, to the organisational power structures of government. The natural current of digital communications is to dismantle the top-heavy world of executive authority in favour of devolution to the local level, or, more simply, to a level at which, glimpsed finally through the eyes of real people in real situations, public meaning becomes possible rather than nominal and abstract.

And yet the conventional wisdom, the standards in good practice, give precious little time and space in which to foster or cultivate the rounded characters and identities of real people in real situations. In its transitory and evanescent form, everything online is reduced to a temporary blip, in which, at the most, we see a brief glimpse of the human world that the intricate nexus of connections almost unconsciously wants to reveal or unveil.

So does the conventional wisdom not need challenging? The internet, like our political institutions, is trying to perform an impossible task: democracy tries to represent the interests of many through a few, and digital rhetoric tries to appeal to everyone (or as many people as possible) by making its content wafer thin. Both are products of the same way of thinking.

And just as, almost of its own volition, the tendency of the internet is to democratise power by giving greater access to it, surely the conclusion for digital rhetoric must be, in contrast to the conventional wisdom, not to pare things down, but rather to fill them out. Digital technology, as we have seen and as countless articles and books testify, provides ever-more powerful ways to make sense of things. It allows us to see the wrinkles in the skin of the world, to hear perspectives that might otherwise pass unnoticed. This is the cryptic and circumstantial soul of things about which Plato writes with such force and structured elegance in *Phaedrus*.

Rather than stripping down an impersonal message to its most primitive essentials in order to position it where the eye is looking, should we not try to illuminate the surprise and contrasts of every possible human story? The internet does not need to become more fast-paced, more competitive, slick, streamlined and concise; it needs more humanity, which is to say identity, terrain, character, art, insight, tradition, iconography; in short, more culture. The picture it presents does not need condensing to a point of vanishing; it needs enlarging to a point where we can actually begin to discern something more featured. We should be drawing on technology to create something similar to the probing and powerful form of reportage that Orwell produced in books like *The Road to Wigan Pier*, and *Down and Out in Paris and London*. Orwell shows that with little more than a typewriter and the right attitude you can shine a powerful light on questions of social justice. How much more powerful should the internet be, with the right valence of elements?

There are certainly no shortage of issues, and no shortage of individuals and organisations who care about them. Inequality, poverty, healthcare, the environment, education, international development – all these and more have champions, advocates, political lobbyists, but many of them, when they communicate online, do so in the same way, which creates a sort of monotonous dirge rather than a spine-tingling aria. It is striking that, despite the available data, research not to mention budgets and human resource devoted to some of these issues, a powerful story told through Orwell's eyes is more forceful and memorable than the 140-character facts and blog posts that evaporate into nothing on a daily, almost hourly, basis.

Through successive algorithm updates Google has sought to find ways in which to deliver more meaningful results to the particular interests of individuals trawling through the internet. Google wants to discover people and their character in a vast, a global, glut of information. It has become more and more of an artificial editor. The more it achieves its aim, and the more digital rhetoric follows its example, the more we might negotiate a meaningful political, which is to say moral and truthful, reckoning; the more, you might say, we will recognise the "many" in the "one".

Selected reading

The following is a list of works either cited directly or which have loosely informed the broad theme of these essays.

Aquinas, St.Thomas (trans. Kevin White and Edward. M. Macierowski). 2005. *Commentaries on Aristotle's "On Sense and What is Sensed" and "On Memory and Recollection"*, The Catholic University of America Press

Aristotle (trans. Hugh Lawson-Tancred). 1991. *The Art of Rhetoric*, Penguin

Barnes, Jonathan (ed.). 1995. *The Cambridge Companion to Aristotle*, Cambridge University Press

Belloc, Hilaire. 1913. *The Servile State*, Liberty Fund

Blond, Phillip. 2010. *Red Tory: How Left and Right Have Broken Britain and How We Can Fix It*, faber and faber

Bronk, Richard. 2009. *The Romantic Economist: Imagination in Economics* , Cambridge University Press

Cicero. (trans. E.W. Sutton). 1942. *On the Orator*, Loeb Classical Library, Harvard University Press

[Cicero] (trans. Harry Caplan). 1954. *Rhetorica Ad Herennium*, Loeb Classical Library, Harvard University Press

Dickens, A.G. 1974. *German Nation and Martin Luther*, Hodder & Stoughton

Dunn, John. 2005. *Setting the People Free: The Story of Democracy*, Atlantic Books

Eco, Umberto (trans. Hugh Bredin). 1986. *Art and Beauty in the Middle Ages*, Yale University Press

Eco, Umberto and Carrière, Jean-Claude (trans. Polly McLean). 2012 *This is Not the End of the Book: A conversation curated by Jean-Philippe de Tonnac*, Vintage

Eisenstein, Elizabeth L. 1983. *The Printing Revolution in Early Modern Europe*, Cambridge University Press

Geary, Ian and Pabst, Adrian (eds). 2015. *Blue Labour: Forging a new politics*, I.B. Tauris

Gierke, Otto (trans. Frederic William Maitland). 1900. *Political Theories of the Middle Age*, Cambridge University Press

Gill, Eric. 1933. *Beauty Looks After Herself*, Angelico Press

Gray, John. 1995. *Enlightenment's Wake*, Routledge

Guignon, Charles (ed.). 1993. *The Cambridge Companion to Heidegger*, Cambridge University Press

Hampson, Norman. 1968. *The Enlightenment: An evaluation of its assumptions, attitudes and values*, Penguin

Heidegger, Martin (ed. David Farrell Krell). 1978. *Basic Writings*, Routledge

Hilton, Steve. 2015. *More Human: Designing a World Where People Come First*, Penguin

Hobbes, Thomas (ed. John Gaskin). 1996. *Leviathan*, Oxford University Press

Lane, Melissa. 2014. *Greek and Roman Political Ideas*, Penguin

- 2001. *Plato's Progeny: How Plato and Socrates still captivate the modern mind*, Duckworth

Leith, Sam. 2012. *You Talkin' To Me?: Rhetoric from Aristotle to Obama*, Profile Books

MacIntyre, Alasdair. 1981. *After Virtue*, Duckworth

MacCulloch, Diarmaid. 2004. *Reformation: Europe's House Divided 1490-1700*, Penguin

Maritain, Jacques. 2007. *Art and Scholasticism with Other Essays*, Filiquarian Publishing, LLC

Mayer-Schonberger, Viktor and Cukier, Kenneth. 2013. *Big Data: A Revolution That Will Transform How We Live, Work and Think*, John Murray

Milbank, John. 1997. *The Word Made Strange: Theology, Language, Culture*, Blackwell

- 1990. *Theology and Social Theory*, Blackwell

Murdoch, Iris. 1970. *The Sovereignty of Good*, Routledge & Kegan Paul

Nuttall, A.D. 2007. *Shakespeare the Thinker*, Yale University Press

- 1967. *Two Concepts of Allegory: A Study of Shakespeare's The Tempest and the Logic of Allegorical Expression*, Yale University Press

Orwell, George. 1968. *Essays*, Penguin

- .2014. *The Road to Wigan Pier*, Penguin

- .2001. *Down and Out in Paris and London*, Penguin

Pattison, George. 2005. *Thinking About God in an Age of Technology*, Oxford University Press

- .2000. *The Later Heidegger*, Routledge

- .1998. *Art, Modernity and Faith: Restoring the Image*, SCM Press

Pickstock, Catherine. 1998. *After Writing: On the Liturgical Consummation of Philosophy*, Blackwell

Plato. (trans. Robin Waterfield). 1994. *Gorgias*, Oxford University Press

- . (trans. Robin Waterfield). 2002. *Phaedrus*, Oxford University Press

- . (trans. Robin Waterfield). 1993. *Republic*, Oxford University Press

Polanyi, Karl. 1944. *The Great Transformation: The Political and Economic Origins of Our Time*, Beacon Press

Self, Will. 2014. *A Point of View: Why Orwell was a literary mediocrity*, BBC Magazine, http://www.bbc.co.uk/news/magazine-28971276

Shakespeare, William (ed. G.R. Hibbard). 1990. *Love's Labour's Lost*, Oxford University Press

Schmidt, Eric and Cohen, Jared. 2014. *The New Digital Age: Reshaping the Future of People, Nations and Business*, John Murray

Siedentop, Larry. 2014. *Inventing the Individual: The Origins of Western Liberalism*, Allen Lane

Strauss, Leo. 1964. *The City and Man*, The University of Chicago Press

Tapscott, Don and Williams, Anthony D. 2006. *Wikinomics*, Atlantic Books

Toulmin, Stephen. 1992. *Cosmopolis: The Hidden Agenda of Modernity*, The University of Chicago Press

Vyvyan, John. 1959. *The Shakespearean Ethic*, Shepheard-Walwyn (Publishers) Ltd

Yates, Frances. 1966. *The Art of Memory*, Pimlico

Zuckert, Catherine H. 1996. *Postmodern Platos*, The University of Chicago Press

Websites

I encounter relevant articles about digital communications almost every day, which means they are too
numerous to list (or even remember!). But some of the
regular sources for these articles include:

A list Apart
http://alistapart.com/topics/content/

Content Marketing Institute
http://contentmarketinginstitute.com/blog/

Content Science
http://review.content-science.com/

The Conversation - Chartered Institute of Public
Relations
http://conversation.cipr.co.uk/

Econsultancy Digital Marketing Blog
https://econsultancy.com/blog/

Forrester's Blogs
http://blogs.forrester.com/

Government Digital Service
https://gds.blog.gov.uk/

Guardian Data Blog
http://www.theguardian.com/data

Guardian Technology Blog
http://www.theguardian.com/technology/blog

Less Work, More Flow
http://urbinaconsulting.com/blog/

Mashable
http://mashable.com/

Sticky Content
http://www.stickycontent.com/blog/

Nielsen Norman Group
http://www.nngroup.com/articles/